AF651864

LEARNING TO SHARE

VOLUME-ONE

Learning to Share Series

Volume One: Learning to Share: Experiences and Reflections on PRA and Community Participation/ *Neela Mukherjee, Vinita Kumar, Meera Jayaswal* and *Bratindi Jena*

Volume Two: Learning to Share: Experiences and Reflections on PRA and Other Participatory Approaches/ *Neela Mukherjee* and *Bratindi Jena*

Volume Three: Learning to Share: Experiences and Reflections on Participatory Approaches/ *Neela Mukherjee* and *Rupa Dasgupta*

About the Editors

The book has been edited by a team of editors from the SRIJ group on participatory development which is an informal and a non-funded group of professionals involved in participatory development. The SRIJ group cuts across different disciplines, organizations and work areas. Amongst the team of editors, **Dr. Neela Mukherjee**, Professor of Economics, LBS National Academy of Administration, Mussoorie is involved as a facilitator and an action researcher in Participatory Rural Appraisal, **Dr. Vinita Kumar**, presently working as Director in the Ministry of Rural Areas and Employment, has considerable experience in rural poverty and participatory policy approaches, **Dr. Meera Jayaswal**, currently working as Assistant Director in Population Education Resource Centre at Ranchi University, Ranchi, Bihar has been involved in application of participatory approaches to primary education and reproductive health of tribals and **Dr. Bratindi Jena**, research officer at the Institute of Development Studies at Jaipur is currently engaged with gender and livelihood issues at the field level.

LEARNING TO SHARE

Experiences and Reflections on PRA and Community Participation

VOLUME-ONE

Edited by
NEELA MUKHERJEE
VINITA KUMAR
MEERA JAYASWAL
BRATINDI JENA

CONCEPT PUBLISHING COMPANY PVT. LTD.
NEW DELHI-110059

© Editors

All rights reserved. No part of this work may be reproduced, stored, adapted, or transmitted in any form or by any means, electronic, mechanical, photocopying, micro-filming recording or otherwise, or translated in any language, without the prior written permission of the copyright owner and the publisher. The book is sold subject to the condition that it shall not, by way of trade or otherwise, be lent, resold, hired out, or otherwise circulated without the prior publisher's written consent in any form of binding or cover other than that in which it is published.

The views and opinions expressed in this book are editor(s) own and the facts reported by him/her have been verified to the extent possible, and the publishers are not in any way liable for the same.

ISBN: 978-81-7022-664-2 (Vol. 1)
ISBN: 978-81-7022-663-5 (Series)

First Published 1997

Published and Printed by

Concept
Since 1974

Concept Publishing Company Pvt. Ltd.
A/15-16, Commercial Block, Mohan Garden,
New Delhi-110059 (India)
T : 91-11-41101460
E : publishing@conceptpub.com, *W*: www.conceptpub.com

EDITORIAL

With gradual shift in development paradigm from the "top down" blueprint-oriented system to "bottom-up" participatory approach, a galaxy of innovative efforts are emerging at the field level. Many professionals are changing their earlier stance and behaviour and are adopting participatory learning methodologies at the field level to interact with local communities and learn from them. Such participatory learning by professionals are taking place under diverse conditions in multitude of ways which are relatively unstructured, flexible and innovative. It is in this context that the present book provides an opportunity to share some of the participatory learning experiences and reflections of a group of professionals who are engaged in embracing the paradigm shift taking place in the sphere of development.

Diverse Community Participation and Empowerment

Today, community participation is at the centre stage of development activities, although the ways, means and practice of such participation vary widely. In some places, local community participates (whether self-initiated or otherwise) to set its own development agenda and act on that basis, while at other places, local communities are consulted on a pre-determined development agenda of an outside agency for soliciting participation. Sometimes participation by local communities is limited to gaining material incentives provided by developmental agencies like wage or food for work and on other occasions, mere information giving by local communities is also termed as participation, often, for investigative research purposes, where local community members analyse and explain their own problems, priorities and solutions, which need not necessarily lead to action at the community and other levels. Hence the degree, quality and methods of community participation vary from one end to the other, not all types of community participation being truly empowering. So is "our" learning from interactive community participation based on community's own developmental priorities which is qualitatively different from that of community participating in plans and schemes designed and implemented by "us" as outside development agencies.

Cumulative Learning and Participation as a Continuum

Community participation can be visualized in terms of a continuum where the process starts from one end of the continuum and gradually progresses over time. If we consider the goal of participatory development to bring about people's empowerment then it is important to appreciate that people's empowerment is a continuum and so is our participatory learning associated with it. Movement from one end of the participatory continuum to the other end, people's empowerment and our cumulative learning are all over a time frame varying from situation to situation. Under such circumstances, continuous reflection helps in enriching the quality of such cumulative learning. Such learning experience also provides a crucial link in progressing towards community empowerment and sustainable development.

Sharing Enriches Learning Process

In contrast to the conventional paradigm encouraging stereotyped "cut and paste" formula and unique solutions to community development, the emphasis of the changed development paradigm is on "learning-by-doing". We as development practitioners when unfolding the new paradigm are getting richer in experience through field learning, and it is important that such experiental learning gets documented for sharing it with larger audience. Documentation, reporting and writing of such experience are important for varied reasons, such as,

- — learning and retaining what is learnt from one's own experience,
- — sharing of learning experience with others,
- — critical reflection on one's own learning
- — open review of learning processes, and
- — enriching it through iteration and validation.

In the ultimate analysis, all such aspects, enrich the quality of participation in development. The issues discussed in such documentation act as feedbacks and clarification for others involved in participatory development. Such learning, sharing, reflection and review help in enriching the process of participation in terms of quality and depth.

Some Limits Posed to Inventory of Participatory Learning

However, such ideal situation is not always forthcoming in many quarters. It often happens that many of our field learnings get recorded in diaries as rough notes, mostly remain un-disseminated and often gather dust on shelves in remote corners. We also find from experience that some of our field learnings get processed into governmental/non-governmental reports, stacked in obscure places which remain inaccessible to many. Although, as practitioners, some of our anecdotes get transmitted from one corner to another by word of mouth, many aspects of participatory process keep accumulating in our minds and it is not unnatural for us to discover that, over time, a part or whole of our mental stock gets diminished or blurred for lack of proper opportunities for sharing with others. Often, we have valid reasons such as lack of time, opportunities and ways which deter us from documenting our experience and sharing them with others. However, all such learning experience, thoughts and reflections when not shared with others and not documented systematically are lost from the invaluable inventory of participatory learning which constitutes a critical link in the on-going process of development experience. Hence, documentation and dissemination constitute integral parts of such learning.

Field Learning and Dissemination

The very paradigm of participatory development has created space for unstructured and open-ended learning process and there is taking place a lot of reversal of "structured" learning for professionals engaged in the field of participatory development. Given such opportunities for learning and reflection, the importance of dissemination, documentation and sharing has assumed great significance. In this direction, a small group, informal and unfunded, was formed in late 1996 by the name of 'SRIJ' group, cutting across organizations and professions involved in the area of participatory learning. The primary objective of SRIJ group is to embark on publishing papers and notes on participatory developmental learning. Towards this end, the present book is the first volume of the group containing collection of papers and notes on participatory learning.

Papers in this Volume

Many of the SRIJ members have contributed towards this edited book in addition to those by other professionals involved in this area. The outcome is a collection of papers and notes on the subject of participatory approaches and learnings. While some of the papers relate to Participatory Rural Appraisal (PRA), others combine Rapid Rural Appraisal (RRA) and PRA, some are also based on participatory research methodology while others combine direct observation with participatory methods.

All papers and notes in this book are based on participatory learning from field situation occurring in the natural context. They have been arranged on the basis of their focus on local communities and societal groups. To start with it is important to have an overview of the paradigm shift in development interventions. Towards this end Mahesh Chander's paper on "PRA, Participatory Extension and Sustainable Agricultural Development: Theory, Practice and Implications" provides an overview of such change and its implications. It traces the shift in developmental paradigm from the "top-down" approach to people's participation based on PRA and participatory agricultural extension. The paper draws from field experience, existing literature, meetings, conferences, events and development agendas of developmental agencies to describe major developmental issues. It highlights how RRA/PRA approach is different from other methods of social inquiry since it cannot ignore the poorest of the poor. Such informal methods of inquiry have helped many professionals in changing stereotyped images about rural life and conditions and made their approach realistic and practical by establishing communication channels with people. The paper discusses how with two existing schools of thought, the "bottom-up" and the "top-down" approaches, many developing countries have now two extension systems, one of which is participatory and the other conventional, where efforts are being made to integrate farmer's knowledge with formal research. The paper argues that the problems of poverty, hunger, malnutrition and disease can be redressed through participatory development by developing stronger linkages with rural communities.

The disadvantaged societal groups like children, women poor and tribals are of paramount importance and participatory learning methodologies can provide insights and understanding of the issues related to such groups. Children's participation being the focal point of Bratindi Jena's paper "Applying PRA Techniques to Child—

Related Issues", it analyses the perceptions and expressions of a group children from Dosra Khurd, a rural village of Rajasthan, in order to learn about their dreams, problems and daily workload. From the children's drawing of items of their choice the author was able to learn about their present living status vis-a-vis dreams and wishes and subsequently, from further discussions their problems and daily workload were also identified. Gender differences surfaced in such expressions of children, where boys aspired for power and were relatively vocal as compared to girls who were over-loaded with daily work and were quite reluctant to communicate.

Meera Jayaswal's paper "Participatory Teaching-Learning Process in Primary Education" shows how adoption of participatory teaching-learning process can lead to better quality of educational attainment in language and mathematics, thereby improving the performance of children in the formative stage of schooling. Such participatory teaching-learning process was based on topics related to their activities and stories, songs, experience, events, objects and materials which were familiar to children. The study relates to schools from six villages situated in rural areas of Ranchi in Bihar.

Indira Kohli's paper "Hidden Agenda" is a story of marginalised poor women who were excluded while benefits from developmental programmes were being shared by local community members. The paper describes how such women when given a chance to voice their opinion were able to express it in a beneficial manner. Frequent contacts, persistent and gentle confidence building help such poor women to come close and participate. Economic gain is of priority consideration for such women group and income generating programmes make them feel confident, develop their managerial skills and help in building other linkages.

In the arena of political participation, women's participation at the grassroots is an integral part of the development process. Mitali Sen Gavai in her paper. "Training for Woman's Political Participation" takes a close look at the process of gender participation emerging as a result of India's Seventy-Third Constitutional Amendment. By means of interviews and case studies of selected women panchayat functionaries the paper describes gender conflict between such functionaries and male vested interests which paralyses the environment for their effective functioning. The paper suggests capacity building of such women functionaries by providing them with training inputs in political education, skills and broadening of vision together with a supportive social environment.

The paper "A Study of Work, Environment and Health of the Rural Women of the Himalayas" by Anjali Bahuguna describes the critical role played by women in the economy of Uttrakhand. With the migration of the youth male workforce to the plains in search of work, the women are left behind in villages to sustain their family in harsh circumstances. With fragmented and scattered land holdings, amidst degradation of land and soil, scarcity of fuel, fodder and water, and limited opportunities of employment in the secondary and tertiary sectors, sustenance of livelihood poses a real challenge. Faced with such odds, the realisation by women themselves of the critical role they can play through collective action for control and management of natural resources holds great promise for better quality of life and sustainable development.

The marginalised and deprived groups of women and children are important as focus groups for participation and so is the community. It is with local community's involvement and effort that enterprises can be sustained and quality of life in local areas can improve with beneficial impacts on different groups within a community. Hari Govind Singh's paper entitled "Community Participation in Kusiyara Watershed Project" describes the extent to which village community of Kusiyara in Mirzapur of Uttar Pradesh participated for identifying local developmental problems. The community also found ways of resolving them by different means including income generation and employment creation by undertaking management of its developmental activities. Such community participation increased awareness of the villagers for minimum wage, generated community funds, increased women's participation in the project, reduced outside migration and settled land problems of local tribals. The paper also highlights the problems faced during implementation, the errors committed and other learnings about the impact of the programme on different actors on the scene.

Amitava Mukherjee's paper "Community Interactions in Discovery of a Rural Slum" shows how discussions with villagers of village Saddopur in Ghazipur of Uttar Pradesh and their problem-ranking exercise led to an interesting finding of how some typical characteristics of a slum can exist in a rural village although the underlying causes can be vastly different. The paper points out that despite such apparent similarity with urban slum, the underlying causes make for relatively tougher living conditions of rural slum dwellers.

In her paper "Community Development in Indonesia: Some Lessons for India" Vinita Kumar draws comparative lessons for India from the experience of Indonesia and shows how people's involvement, education and right to information and communication have helped communities in Indonesia to sustain benefits of community development programmes. Though traditionally, power flows from "top" to the "bottom", Indonesia has developed several alternative mechanisms for community participation which have facilitated a "bottom-up" approach for effective implementation of community development programmes. Such mechanisms have facilitated a "two-way" communication of message from the government to the people and from the people to the government. Awareness through information, education and communication has ensured maximum participation of community in developmental schemes.

Anil C. Shah in his paper "Developmental PLAs" focuses on the importance of participatory learning and action and direct participation of the beneficiaries in the planned projects. Active participation of communities helps in sustainability of projects where the communities have technical knowledge about the availability of resources, its location, its utility and their need for the same. The author concludes that farmers' organization with a proper network of education, information and communication can make the most of programmes related to irrigation and cultivation.

S.B. Roy, Ganesh Yadav and Raktima Mukherjee in their paper "Process of Conflict Resolution in Participatory Forest Management" describe the causes of societal conflict and the basic steps in conflict management at local levels by means of a case study on participatory forest management in Sarugarh, North Bengal. Resource mapping by local villagers of village Sarugarh enhanced their self-esteem and led to visualization of existing local resources as against their demands. Face-to-face interactions with the community reduced the social distance with forest officials and also helped in negotiations for resolving the conflict situation. The paper shows how empathy and objective concern are essential for resolution of conflict.

Indira Kohli in her story on "Poverty Alleviation and the PRA of Ethics" shows how lack of adequate communication with local groups acts as a lacunae in our poverty alleviation programmes. With the help of a field-based story of a poor household, Kohli shows how need for earning a livelihood controlled and directed decision-making in that poor household which was in conflict with the interests of women of the richer households. Some lessons drawn by Kohli on the basis of the story are that community development programmes should address the issue of basic needs within poor households on a priority basis. Often many intra-community issues remain hidden and do not find opportunities for discussion. Such blockage of information affects community participation, planning and implementation. Hence, there is a need for creating an environment for free and open communication for better sharing of such issues.

Organizations involved in participatory development also require changes in organizational attitudes and behaviour for gearing towards participatory development. Neela Mukherjee's paper "Organizational Capacity Building for Participatory Rural Appraisal PRA: Some Lessons from the field" identifies and discusses selected phases in pro-participatory development approach of organizations and issues in sustainability of such phases.

We wish to thank members of the SRIJ group and other contributors in this book who responded positively by writing about their learnings from field experience. Support towards dissemination of the contents of the book by PRA Network at the Institute of Development Studies at Sussex is gratefully acknowledged, thanks are due to Kamal Singh in particular.

We also express our sincere thanks to Ashok Kumar Mittal of Concept Publishing Company for taking keen interest in publication of this book.

The book is meant for all those professionals working in the area of participatory development, whether governmental or non-governmental. The book draws its strength from learnings by different professionals in diverse areas of community participation to show that such learning is quick, open, cumulative, practical, creative and enriching leading to knowledge reversals, opening of thought processes, generating new and innovative ideas, contributing towards policy-making and bridging formidable gaps in our knowledge systems.

Neela Mukherjee,Delhi
Vinita Kumar, Delhi
Meera Jayaswal, Ranchi
Bratindi Jena, Jaipur

CONTENTS

COMMUNITY INTERACTIVE PROCESSES
APPROACHES AND INSIGHTS

THE MORAL FABRIC OF COMMUNITY
PARTICIPATION—ETHICS AND VALUES

ORGANIZATIONAL CAPACITY BUILDING

CONTRIBUTOR'S PROFILE

Dr. Mahesh Chander

Dr. Mahesh Chander is Agricultural graduate (BSc Ag. & AH) with post-graduate qualifications in Agricultural Communication and Extension (M.Sc) and Ph.D. (Extension Education) from premier institutions of Agricultural Education and Research (G.B. Pant University of Agriculture and Technology, Pantnagar, and Indian Veterinary Research Institute (IVRI), Izatnagar. He has been working as Agricultural Research Service scientist with the Indian Council of Agricultural research (ICAR) in the discipline of Agricultural extension. As a part of his research and field extension activities, he has done action research and thus, has field experience in participatory extension and development. The field extension work in the rural areas of Kumaon hills brought him closer to the hill farmers who gave him lot of understanding about the grassroot realities as faced by the hill farmers and women. He has contributed a number of papers and articles on these issues in large number of journals. His current interests include sustainable agricultural development including organic farming and participatory extension activities.

Dr. Bratindi Jena

Dr. Bratindi Jena is a trained Psychologist. She obtained Ph. D. in Psychology from Delhi University in 1995. She worked with Women Producers of Kumaon hills for three years on an action project. She also did a project on Women and Mental Health. At present she is involved in a participatory policy research programme at IDS Jaipur.

Dr. Meera Jayaswal

Dr. Meera Jayaswal has doctorate degree in Educational Psychology and D. Litt. degree in Health Psychology. She is currently Assistant

Director in Population Education Resource Centre at Ranchi University, Ranchi, Bihar. She is also associated with Bihar Education Project Council, Patna, Bihar as State Resource Person and Working in the area of quality improvement of primary education. Her research interest include application of participatory approach in primary education of children, adolescent education of adolescents and health-population education of adolescents, tribals and women.

Indira Kohli

Dr. Indira Kohli is a consultant on community participation through the PRA process. She was the Founder of the ONGC Himalayan Association, founder President of the ONGC Mahila Polytechnic and the four associated Rural Polytechnics. She is a member of the Governing Council Indian Mountaineering Foundation, President of the Society for Resource Sustainability, and is at present a consultant on Community Participation with the Watershed Management Directorate, Forest Department UP.

Mitali Sen Gavai

Mitali Sen Gavai is an officer of the Maharashtra State Cadre of the Indian Administrative Service. Her present assignment involves training officials and non-officials at YASHADA, the state training institute. Ms. Gavai is especially engaged in addressing the special learning needs of the women functionaries of the panchayat institutions of self-governance in rural Maharashtra.

Dr. Anjali Bahuguna

Dr. Anjali Bahuguna is employed as Reader in the Department of Economics, H.B.B. Garhwal University, Srinagar (Garhwal) in Uttar Pradesh. She has research experience of over 20 years and has edited a book entitled "Science and Technology in Relation to Rural Women", Har Anand Publications, New Delhi, 1995. She is deeply involved in empowerment of hill women of Garhwal. She also has a large number of research papers to her credit.

Dr. Harigovind Singh

Dr. Harigovind Singh is working as Assitant Director of Arthik Anusandhan Kendra, a reputed NGO involved at the grassroots. He started working for the cause of under-priviledged "kol" community in close with Dr. Kripa Shankar from the year 1991. Today, with active participation of team of one hundred social activists such work has spread in fifty villages. Working in a team of dedicated individuals, Dr. Hari Govind Singh remains committed to his team, the ideologies pursued and to the mission of his organization.

Dr. Amitava Mukherjee

Dr. Amitava Mukherjee is a noted economist and currently the Executive Director of ACTION AID India, one of the largest international non-governmental funding organizations in India. Dr. Mukherjee has written extensively on Participation, Rural Development and Micro-Level Planning. He has 25 books and many papers on the above subject to his credit."

Dr. Vinita Kumar

Dr. Vinita Kumar, a member of the Indian Economic Service, is presently working as Director in the Ministry of Rural Areas and Employment. She has acquired varied field experience in rural poverty and participatory process through her work experience in the Ministry of Rural Areas and Employment, for the last five years. She received her Ph. D. degree in Economics from Lucknow University. She has many published papers to her credit including a book entitled *Economic Growth and Rural Poverty: The Indian Experience (1960-95)* by Concept Publishing Company, Delhi.

Anil C. Shah

Anil Shah has been active in the field of development, particularly rural development since the launching of Community Development in India in 1952. As a member of Indian Administrative Service, he has worked at Block, District, State and National level. After his retirement from Government service, he worked as the Chief Executive of Aga Khan Rural Support Programme (India) which has become a leading NGO in the country in the field of natural resources development. At present, he is the Chairman of the Development Support Centre, an NGO founded by him in 1994, for providing support to voluntary organisations entering the area of natural resources development. Anil Shah is a learner and practitioner of participatory development on which he writes regularly.

Prof. S. B. Roy

Professor S. B. Roy is Ph.D., Anthropology and has served for 22 years as researcher in Anthropological Survey of India, Government of India. He has conducted training programmes for Indian Forest Service Officers, Civil Servants, engineers and others bureaucrats, planners in India, China, Indonesia, Nepal, U.K.

He is presently Professor of Indian Institute of Technology, Vinod Gupta School of Management, Kharagpur, India and founder Chairman, Indian Institute of Bio-Social Research and Development (IBRAD), Calcutta, India. He has edited/authored number of books/research articles on Joint Forest Management.

Ganesh Yadav and Raktima Mukherjee

Both Ganesh Yadav and Raktima Mukherjee are programme officers of IBRAD, Calcutta and have acquired great competency and field experience in the subject of participatory forest management. Both are involved in different training programmes on Joint Forest Management and action research of IBRAD.

Dr. Neela Mukherjee

Dr. Neela Mukherjee is currently employed as Professor of Economics at Lal Bahadur Shastry National Academy of Administration, Mussoorie (Uttar Pradesh), India. Dr. Mukherjee's major area of research lies in participatory development in which she has written extensively. Her books include *Participatory Appraisal of Natural Resources* (1997), *Paticipatory Rural Appraisal: Methodology and Applications* (1993) and *Participatory Rural Appraisal and Questionnaire Survey (Comparative Field Experience and Methodological Innovations)* (1995) published by Concept Publishing Company, Delhi. Dr. Mukherjee has long experience of conducting training programmes for governmental, non-governmental and donor agencies in the areas of participatory rural appraisal, project sustainability, participatory monitoring and evaluation, participatory health need assessment etc.

MEMBERS OF 'SRIJ' GROUP, 1996

Sri Abhijit Ghose
IFS, Conservator of Forests (Project Formulation & Evaluation), Jaipur (Rajasthan).

Ms. Bindu Kalia
Joint Secretary, Rural Litigation & Entitlement Kendra, Dehradun (U.P.).

Dr. Hari Govind Singh
Assistant Director, Arthik Anusandhan Kendra, Allahabad (U.P.).

Dr. Indira Kohli
President, Resource Sustainability Through Community Participation, Dehradun (U.P.).

Sri K.C. Thapliyal
(ex-IFS), Chairman, Resource Sustainability Through Community Participation, Dehradun (U.P.).

Dr. Kanchan Chopra
Professor, Institute of Economic Growth, Delhi.

Ms. Mamta Mukherjee
Economist, Development Alternatives, New Delhi.

Dr. Meera Jayaswal
Assistant Director, Population Education Resource Centre, Ranchi (Bihar).

Ms. Mitali Sen-Gavai
IAS Director, Parishraman, Yashada, Pune (Maharashtra).

Sri N.K. Banerjee
Deputy Director, Centre for Women's Development Studies, New Delhi.

Dr. Neela Mukherjee
Professor of Economics, LBS National Academy of Administration, Mussoorie (U.P.).

Sri Pawan Kumar Gupta
Director, Society for Integrated Development of Himalayas, Mussoorie (U.P.).

Dr. Vinita Kumar

IES, Director, Ministry of Rural Areas and Employment, New Delhi.

Dr. Anjali Bahuguna

Reader, Department of Economics, Hemvati Nandan Bahuguna University, Srinagar, Garhwal (U.P.).

Dr. Bratindi Jena

Research Officer, Institute of Development Studies, Jaipur (Rajasthan).

THEORY AND PRACTICE OF SHIFTING PARADIGM

1

PRA AND PARTICIPATORY EXTENSION
Theory, Practice and Implications

— MAHESH CHANDER

In 1996-97, two international conferences were held in India where, perhaps for the first time, the farmers from the grassroots had a say while sharing platform with the international experts in agricultural sciences and rural development. First, International Crop Sciences Congress, held at Indian Agricultural Research Institute (IARI), New Delhi in November, 1996 and second, International Conference on Creativity and Innovation at Grassroots for Sustainable Natural Resources Management held at Indian Institute of Management (IIM), Ahmedabad in January, 1997. These two events are significant not only for their magnitude and range of issues discussed but for the participation of the farmers and grassroot innovators who could share their experiences, problems, prospects and potential for agricultural development with free and frank discussions in a participatory environment. The conference at IIM particularly emphasized the farmer experimentations, innovations and creativity at grassroots with large number of farmers in attendance from different corners of India. In fact, the conference itself was inaugurated by a grassroot innovator Sri Amrut Bhai Agravat. Such changes in the character of conferences is a departure from the tradition of highly technical paper presentations mostly by the lab oriented experts before the scientific community. The question arise, why this departure from the routine? The answer is obvious, the traditional approach of top down development and centralized planning over the years could not solve the problems of poverty, hunger, malnutrition, illiteracy and disease from the society to a significant extent leading to the frustration, restlessness and finally to rethinking about development planning.

Internationally, the concerns were voiced mainly by the social scientists about the developments which were divorced from the realities at the grassroots (Chambers, 1983). The **Farmer First** (Chambers *et al.*, 1989) was perhaps the first major document which revolutionized the new thinking about development wherein the farmers were brought to the centre stage of development. The **Farmer First** not only generated a debate on the farmers' role in development planning but also paved the way for searching alternatives in social enquiry and forms of development which ensure farmers' participation. RRA/PRA, thus, is the outcome of this new paradigm of development which has attracted tremendous attention from different corners as is evident from the growing body of knowledge in this area.

The traditional approach of agricultural extension has been of Transfer of Technology (TOT) wherein the farmers were supposed to be informed, educated and advised by the extension workers who in turn were in touch with the experts in the research institutions, ideally speaking. Such approach was based on top down transfer of knowledge paradigm often considering the farmers as passive recipient of the knowledge generated by the scientists in the laboratories. The National Extension Services under the Ministries of Agriculture operated with this typical thinking ever since their inception. The Training and Visit (T&V) system of extension is a classic example of such an approach which was generously funded by The World Bank and readily adopted by many developing countries including India during 1980s. This system of extension was considered to the superior to other existing extension systems being more streamlined yet the outcome was not very encouraging rather being questioned now, after of course, spending billions of rupees. After all, this is not the isolated case where the development funding could not bring about desired results. The rethinking in development process and funding as well at the level of international agencies like FAO, The World Bank, WHO besides other development agencies and donors in favour of participatory form of development is not without a price since these bodies had spent billions before such thinking got a foothold. Now the emphasis is on farmer participation, rural peoples' knowledge, traditional wisdom, for the sake of sustainable development.

The World Conference on Agrarian Reforms and Rural Development (WCARRD) in Rome in 1979 was the landmark since FAO, World Bank, WHO and many other government agencies and NGOs realized the need for more participatory, people focussed approach in place of long established external, professionally led styles of project interventions. The WCARRD heavily emphasized the role of people's participation forcing the world bodies to redesign their developmental interventions. The much of re-thinking at the levels of UN agencies is attributed to this important conference. Besides, Robert Chambers argued that there is a need to replace the transfer of technology (TOT) model of extension because of its link with top-down conceptions of change such as the adoption of innovation and the process of diffusion (Chambers, 1990). Also, it has been argued (Kloppenburg, 1991) that agricultural problems should be approached from local knowledge bases and that alternative agricultural systems could be enhanced by cooperation between biological and social scientists. The new extension theories are also influenced by the work of Rhoades and Booth (1982) who used the term 'farmer-back-to-farmer' to depict the notion that the research activities should begin and end with the farmer. This thinking was later developed into **'Farmer-First'** (Chambers, 1990), **'Putting People First'** (Cernea,1991) and **'Farmer Participatory Research'** (Farrington and Martin, 1988). These approaches have been put in use in the form of Rapid Rural Appraisal (RRA) and Participatory Rural Appraisal (PRA). All these developments emerged on the notion of an alternative extension approach to TOT and thus, collectively known as 'bottom- up' extension, the best described now as 'farmer- first'.

The Institute of Development Studies (IDS) at University of Sussex, UK; Sustainable Agriculture Programme of International Institute of Environment and Development (IIED), London; Overseas Development Institute (ODI), UK; Khon Kaen University, Thailand to name a few have brought out a large number of publications on PRA and participatory development, thus contributing and adding to the knowledge on the issue. The book, **Beyond Farmer First** (Scoones and Thompson, 1994) has further advanced the debate on farmer participatory research and extension practice. The development of agricultural extension in the third world in the next few years is likely to revolve around the ideological debates provoked by this trend even though many extensionists suspect the debate is already well ahead of actual practice in the field (Oakley, 1994).

The participatory form of extension is still largely in the domain of NGOs and other informal networks like women's groups, cooperatives, rural unions which are said to be doing better extension service to the small farmers in comparison to the traditional top down official forms of agricultural extension. As such two types of agricultural extension systems are in operation in developing countries which often criticize each other for their comparative relevance, importance and impacts. The top down mentality obviously dominates as it is firmly imbedded in the minds of many administrators. To many, the farmer participatory research and extension is a concept talked more than actually acted upon because researchers, scientists and administrators are reluctant to give over control to farmers. Whereas, a growing number of professionals now realize that the genuine farmer participatory research has the potential to make a significant contribution to feeding the world. Releasing that potential is the task of people of many disciplines concerned for sustainable development. It is in this context, farmer participatory research has rightly generated considerable excitement in recent times.

The growing body of literature suggest that a substantial "re-think" appears to have occurred, in theory at least, and the word participation is creeping into the vocabulary of many extension activities. Especially at international donors level, concerted and genuine efforts are being made to institutionalize this "new thinking" and inject fresh ideas into National Extension Services (Oakley, 1994). This is evident from the fact that the FAO has come out with the fresh texts (Axinn, 1988; Adhikarya, 1994) on extension whereby the participatory extension has been adequately emphasized. Besides, several other international development agencies, agricultural universities and research institutions are re-orienting their approach in favour of participatory research and extension which is reflected by the literature published by them. As far as the methodological contributions on PRA and its field applications are concerned, the studies in rural participation series (Mukherjee, 1993, 1995) figure prominently in Indian context which are likely to be followed by many organizations. This series may in fact serve as a main guiding force for participatory research and development in agricultural sector of developing countries in general. The reports on field applications of PRA methodologies are increasingly available from mainly the NGOs. These theoretical as well as practical experiences on participatory research and extension are likely to shape the agricultural development scenario of developing countries in coming years with the joining of the public sector agencies in this sort of development.

The developments are not only taking place in the matters of theory and publications but the institutions including the government ones have started taking action upon the participatory paradigm of development. The PRA type inquiry based methodologies are now increasingly being adopted by many government agencies in India besides the NGOs (MYRADA, AKRSP, Action Aid for example) which have already established a lead in this area. To name a few, The National Dairy Development Board (NDDB), National Institute for Management of Agricultural Extension (MANAGE), National Institute of Rural Development (NIRD) and Indian Council of Agricultural Research (ICAR, Singh and Schiere, 1994a, for example). Besides, many agricultural universities are now following PRA approach as is evident from the training activities going on in these institutions. The watershed development projects are following this approach in a big way. The international donor emphasis and support, however, is one important motivating factor for the development of PRA based development activities in most of the cases in developing countries including India.

It would be very pertinent here to quote verbatim a joint foreword message by Dr. R.S. Paroda (Director General, ICAR) and others for a technical bulletin (Singh and Schiere, 1994). They said, much of the extension work in crops and livestock development in the past, in India and elsewhere, was based on the assumption that researchers and government officials could tell the farm family how to improve their mode of agriculture and subsequently their income ! Experience thus far has taught, however, that particularly in the farming systems with high variations between farms, it is difficult to suggest a new technology or management practice without incorporating farmers' suggestions and observations that can help improve the innovation. Whereas, the scientific community has mainly focussed on the biological responses of animals and crops, and the extension community has focussed on increased output per animal or hectare, it is ultimately the farm family that decides on the basis of their own perception of profit and risk. It is in this context RRA hold promise which focus on local problems and farmer perceptions, they said further. This forward message has clearly admitted the need of mutual learning between the development workers and farmers. These thoughtful views and realization at the highest level of agricultural research administration from Director General of Indian Council of Agricultural Research (ICAR) who also happens to be Secretary, Department of Agricultural Research and Education (DARE), Government of India are important pointer to significant implications for agricultural development in coming years. This would of course require a genuine desire for change at the lower levels as well. The thinking has to percolate down at the levels of implementation and should be reflected in the functioning of the various institutions under the ICAR, once in principle, PRA and participatory development has been accepted by the headquarters, thus the message is quoted in verbatim.

A review of WCARRD's progress in the 1980s noted that the commitment to participation to date had been more "philosophical" than practical. This seems true since participation implies movement from the grassroots, not all governments or bureaucracies look upon such movements with favour. Traditional extension has reflected the essentially authoritarian rule of officials and bureaucrats. This is where lies the contrast between a typical extension official working with a government department and a NGO extension worker at the operations level. These two are viewed quite differently by the rural poor whom both of them are meant to serve. The expectations of the farmers as well as their opinions are different about these two workers while they are meant for the same job, more or less. One appears to be more formal, full of bureaucratic ego, whereas the other is informal, friendly and often appear as one of them, though exceptions do exist. This is a matter of approach to development which makes a big difference at the operation level. Can it be changed ? The change is a difficult process but certainly not impossible.

Extension is not a matter only of who can and who cannot increase production. It is also a question of reaching the resource poor and marginalized, providing the means and support that make them feel that they are the part of the development process geared to building up the production base. This is to be understood by all those who are providing the extension service to the farmers, be government officials or NGO workers. This is a difficult task. The FAO has been experimenting with this sort of democracy and its experience in participatory extension has included "teething problems" yet great promises have been expected of such participatory efforts (Rouse, 1994) by constantly learning, improving and implementing what is learnt.

Learnings from the Field

Whenever an extension worker or any development official visit rural areas, the very first question he/she encounters is whether they are for any loan scheme or can extend some aid ! Why this happens? This is a big question and speaks a lot about our development planning and administration over the years. For example, a Village Development Officer (VDO) who was called Village Level Worker earlier, is an extension worker at the grassroot level responsible for all development activities including the transfer of technology at village level. How he is perceived by the farmers ? Only as a person who identifies the potential beneficiaries under IRDP or other loan scheme since he is an officer, to be feared by all resource poor farmers and obliged for the favour in terms of the loans. This perception cannot be changed so easily at the grassroots level. The farmers do not bother much for those development officials who do not have any direct financial assurance for them. Here lies a task, much difficult yet not impossible, that is, to bring about change in the rural psyche about the development which is not only in terms of loans but a holistic one. To bring about this change among rural people the development officials themselves will have to bring about change in their own approach of dealing with farmers. This is a challenge to all academicians, researchers, policy planners and practically all those who are for sustainable development.

The experiences of an Action research project on the Integrated development of selected villages in Ramgarh development block in Nainital district of Uttar Pradesh, can be shared here. As soon as this project was taken up as Project Leader by the author, the *Gram Pradhan* (Village head) and other influential groups in the villages tried to find out the financial incentives guaranteed in the project. Once coming close to the multi-disciplinary project team, soon, however, they realized that there were no such direct benefits but indirect ones like mutual sharing of problems, potential, knowledge, besides wider exposure to farmers by arranging their visits to agri-research and development organizations and events like *kisan melas* (farmers' fairs) in the villages itself during four years of action research. This seemed to them something theoretical and not of much significance in comparison to the traditional loan or construction based development activities. Many get discouraged by this initial negative response from the influentials in the villages. These influentials or opinion makers were given important role in traditional TOT model of agricultural extension or even in T&V system of agricultural extension as "contact farmers". Imagine what role they would play on behalf of the majority of resource poor farmers in the villages. The T&V system has been considered more farmer participatory in comparison to the traditional extension systems only because of this component of "contact farmers". Our experience showed that the so called progressive and influential farmers cannot be representative of the other farmers mainly the resource poor majority in the villages yet cannot be ruled out for their role in development planning and implementation in the villages.

The RRA/PRA is an approach which cannot afford to ignore the poorest of poor in the system. This is what *inter alia* makes it a method of social enquiry much different than others. RRA/PRA type enquiry was, therefore, chosen to find out the bench mark information on the villages selected for action research. It required a lot of efforts on the part of the project team to make poor people, women share their views on the problems in the villages. This was challenging yet interesting task which could bring forth may facts which otherwise would never have been known to the scientists involved in the project. For example, the improved grass seeds distributed to the farmers by the government agencies as well as by the NGOs were not sown by the farmers. First, they were reluctant to grow grasses in the small land holding they had; secondly, they knew it for sure that the native grasses growing naturally along the crop fields on the bunds etc. would suppress the unadapted exotic grasses. The Government of Uttar Pradesh as also the several NGOs are spending millions of rupees on introduction of grasses and improved forages in this region but the outcome so far are frustrating at the farmers level. The PRA enquiry revealed poor prospects of the "improved" forage production strategies involving non local grasses and forages.

Buffaloes are growing in number in the hills of Uttar Pradesh yet the available literature on this issue is limited since the experts consider hills as unfavourable locale for buffaloes. The RRA/PRA enquiry in the villages revealed that buffalo is better alternative than the local cows or even cross-bred cattle because of the more fat content in buffalo milk, more manure production capability, ease in disposing off male calf for slaughter, more milk production with locally available inputs. The restricted grazing areas (forests for example) are also the reasons for the farmers' preference for buffaloes vis-a-vis cows as buffaloes are essentially stall fed in hills. The government agencies still consider buffalo as not suitable for hills, hence, there is no significant intervention for the promotion of buffaloes in this region yet the buffaloes are growing in number over cattle. The growing number of village dairy cooperatives in hills are yet another reason for the encouragement to buffalo rearing since dairy cooperatives pay for milk on the basis of fat content. The hill farmers are interested in replacing large number of cows with them to one or two buffaloes given the constraints faced by them in maintaining the cows. The farmers still maintain one or two cows for religious purposes and cow bulls for draught power required in hill agriculture since buffalo bulls are not that efficient. These are the learnings when we enlist farmers' active participation through RRA/PRA types of enquiry. These learnings should be transformed into action to win the confidence of farmers' and to make farmer participatory development a continuous process.

Many development interventions have failed in the past by not achieving the objectives in spite of ambitious targets and massive fundings. The cross-breeding programme is among one such intervention which has so far eluded the developmental agencies in hills of Uttar Pradesh at least. Apart from the infrastructural inadequacies with the animal husbandry department, the sustainability of cross-bred cattle in hills with kind of socio-economic situations and land holding pattern besides input availability makes the craze for cross breeding interventions in this region a questionable strategy (Chander and Mukherjee, 1995; Chander and Harbola, 1996). The RRA type of enquiry may further bring forward many more revealing facts on the cross breeding programmes involving exotic cattle in hills. Therefore, it is important to conduct RRA/PRA before initiating any developmental intervention in any region. The models cannot be replicated everywhere. The local condition make it imperative to make in-depth enquiry jointly by the farmers and development administrators by sharing a common platform and arriving at mutually understood and agreeable solutions. This is what is lacking at programme planning and implementation level in the current system of governance. Imposing a development model standardized and fruitfully applied elsewhere may not be equally rewarding in the larger interest or even may be a big drain on the public exchequer. This fact has to be borne in mind by all those who are responsible for the development at the grassroots. PRAs in addition to RRAs are particularly useful in situations where complex social structures exist, where an institution is considering establishing a long term development programme in a village or region, and where a range of development needs should be addressed (Singh and Schiere, 1994). In nutshell, the perception of the rural people are most important which need due consideration while designing any developmental intervention meant for their development lest their should be chances of failures at the heavy cost of much needed quality of life based development at the grassroots.

Taking a clue from the book on Participatory Rural Appraisal (Mukerjee, 1993), wherein the extension agents have been called upon to learn and gain from the clienteles of their extension work, the informal enquiry as well as the RRAs and PRAs have helped in changing the many stereo typed images about the rural life. This has caused a sense of concern about how theoretical we are, how little we know about the people and their real problems at the grassroots while confining ourselves in the laboratories and offices ? This realization is bound to occur and grow in the minds of many agricultural scientists and researchers confined to the laboratories and experimental farms once they minimise their communication gap with their clientele through participatory research with poor farmers. This would certainly improve the quality of research output which would be more relevant, need based, socially acceptable and sustainable. This is in fact a big challenge to make farmer participatory research and extension a reality proved by the actions at the implementation levels for the larger benefits of mankind lest it should remain a rhetoric.

Concluding Remarks

Participatory development has been enormously emphasised at the international level with ever increasing donor support for such development activities to NGOs as well as government agencies particularly in developing countries in recent times. This emphasis is clearly visible in literature coming out from the international institutions *inter alia* United Nations particularly FAO, Consultative Group on International Agricultural Research (CGIAR), The World Bank, NGOs, universities at national levels as well. This literature has certainly added to the existing knowledge and contributed to the development of theoretical paradigm for ensuring people's participation in development. Besides, the practical information through actual field experiences from the developing countries in Africa, Asia and Latin America may help and guide further improvement in the methodological aspects of participatory development. The echoes of farmers' participation in agricultural technology development and dissemination is also now increasingly heard in national agricultural research and development organizations in developing countries. The debate has generated considerable excitement among the development community and thus the literature is growing on the issues relating to rural participation. To some it is more a philosophical thought than a practical commitment. Putting into practice what has been suggested for genuine farmer participation is a real difficult task particularly for those with traditional top-down mind set of government bureaucracy. But the pressure is equally strong particularly from the proponents of the alternative forms of development led by the NGOs and other informal organizations like farmers' unions, youth and women's organizations who are lobbying for participatory development. The battle lines are drawn, if not in blood at least in ink between "bottom-up" and "top-down" schools of thought. One emphasizing "people's participation", other for "efficiency and quantification". As Oakley (1994) has said, many developing countries now have two extension systems, one participatory and one not. Amid this on-going debate, many organizations have initiated actions giving due recognition to rural people's knowledge, wisdom in solving their own problems. The efforts are now being made to integrate farmers' knowledge with the formal knowledge generated in the agri-research institutions. This is a welcome trend having far reaching implications for sustainable agricultural development.

The theoretical paradigm for participatory development is now sufficiently developed, farmer participation has been considered and accepted important at least in principle by many but the actions on these lines or field applications are still limited with NGOs leading. If taken up by all, GOs and NGOs, the implications of PRA, participatory research and extension are substantial in the matters of feeding the world—a large part of which is still in the grip of poverty, hunger, malnutrition and diseases despite much talked about "Green Revolution" technologies and equally emphasized extension systems like T&V to extend these technologies. The solutions to these problems may be found to a significant extent if the principles and theories of farmer participatory development and PRA are put into practice, sooner the better. The initiatives should now be taken up by people in the fields of research, extension and education to develop stronger linkages with farmers. This will involve new ways of thinking and working, and it is believed that PRA is one methodology which can help. There is also a need for a wider range of people to become involved. These are the views which have emerged from a study (Dunn *et al,* 1996) in Australian context which further concludes that farmers are ready to participate but can the researchers, educators and extension professionals make it happen ? This important question stands to be answered in the context of the other countries as well.

REFERENCES

Adhikarya, Ronny. (1994), *Strategic Extension Campaign : A Participatory Oriented Method of Agricultural Extension:* A Case Study of FAOs Experiences. Agricultural Education and Extension Services (ESHE), Human Resources, institutions and Agrarian Reforms Division of FAO of UN, p. 209.

Axinn, George H., (1988), *Guide on Alternative Extension Approaches.* Agricultural Education and Extension Service (ESHE), Human Resources, Institutions, and Agrarian Reforms Division, FAO of the United Nations, p. 148.

Cernea, M.M. (ed) (1991), *Putting People First : Sociological Variables in Rural Development* (2nd edition). Oxford University Press for the World Bank, New York.

Chambers, Robert, (1983), *Rural Development : Putting the Last First.* London, Longman.

Chambers, R., Pacey, A. and Thrupp, L.A. (1989), *Farmer First : Farmer Innovation and*

Agricultural Research. London, Intermediate Technology Publication.

Chambers, Robert, (1990), Farmer First : A Practical Paradigm for the Third World Agriculture. In Altieri, M.A and Hecht, S.B (eds) *Agro-ecology and Small Farm Development.* CRC Press, Boca Raton.

Chander, Mahesh and Mukherjee, Reena, (1995), *Indigenous Cattle for Sustainability in Himalayan Region of India.* Asian Livestock, xx, 10, November, pp.141-143.

Chander, Mahesh and Harbola, P.C., (1996), *Livestock Management in Himalayan Environment : Constraints, Opportunities and Strategies with Reference to India.* Asian Livestock, xxi, 7, pp.393-408.

Dunn, T., Humphreys, L., Muirhead, W., Plunket, M., Croker, N., and Nickl, M., (1996), Changing Paradigms for Farmer-Researcher-Extensionist Relationships: Exploring Methods and Theories for Farmer Participation in Research. *European Journal of Agricultural Education and Extension,* Vol.3, No.3, December, pp.167-182.

Farrington, J., and Martin, A.M. (1988), *Farmer Participatory Research : A Review of Concepts and Recent Field Work.* Agricultural Administration and Extension, 29, pp.247-264.

Kloppenburg, J., (1991). Social Theory and the De/Reconstruction of Agricultural Science: Local Knowledge for an Alternative Agriculture. *Rural Sociology,* 56, 4, pp.519-548.

Mukherjee, Neela, (1993), *Participatory Rural Appraisal : Methodology and Applications,* Concept Publishing Company, Delhi.

Mukherjee, Neela, (1995), *Participatory Rural Appraisal and Questionnaire Survey* (Comparative field experience and methodological innovations), Concept Publishing Company, Delhi.

Oakley, Peter, (1994), *Bottom-up Versus Top-down : Extension at the Crossroads.* Ceres, The FAO Review No. 145, Vol. 26. No.1, pp. 16-20.

Rhoades, R. and Booth, R., (1982), Farmer-back-to-farmer: A Model for Generating Agricultural Technology. *Agricultural Administration,* 11, pp. 127-137.

Rouse, John, (1994), Experiments with Democracy. Ceres, *The FAO Review* No 145, Vol. 26, no.1, pp.21-25.

Scoones, Ian and Thompson John (eds), (1994), *Beyond Farmer First : Rural Peoples' Knowledge, Agricultural Research and Extension Practice.* London, Intermediate Technology Publications Ltd.

Singh, Kiran and Schiere, J.B. (eds), (1994), On Farm Research for Testing of Appropriate Technologies in Crop-Livestock Production Systems *(ICAR/BIOCON Technical Bulletin No 3).* New Delhi, Indian Council of Agricultural Research (ICAR) and Department of Tropical Animal Production, Wageningen Agricultural University, The Netherlands, p.72.

Singh, Kiran and Schiere, J.B. (eds), (1994a), Rapid Rural Appraisal to assist focussing of research and extension programme for livestock development in India *(ICAR/BIOCON Technical Publication No.2).* New Delhi, ICAR and Wageningen Agricultural University, The Netherlands, p.46.

COMMUNICATING WITH FUTURE STAKEHOLDERS
The Children

2

APPLYING PRA TECHNIQUES TO CHILD RELATED ISSUES

— BRATINDI JENA

Development is a process in itself not an end. What is planned today holds its impact on future generation. However, unfortunately the generation that will bear the fruit of todays development is always neglected or over-looked by the policy makers, economists, planners, donor agencies, NGOs and even their own families. Adult planners don't feel the need to collect information about children because of their own biases. They still perceive children as ignorant, immatured, dependent on adults and take the authority to decide everything on behalf of them. Children's own perceptions are always neglected as immatured and inexperienced. But in this process many issues that are vital for children are overlooked. Very often decisions of adults are forced upon children at every level.

With a fast changing scenario of the present society children no more enjoy an ignorant, dependent and fairy tale childhood. All over the world and particularly in the developing countries childhood is over-burdened with ill-health, poor nutrition, environmental degradation, wants and discrimination. The basic needs of children in almost half of the developing worlds' under five are not met. In India about 63% of children below the age of five years are under-nourished (Deshpande, 1996).

If we talk of sustainable development we need to include children in our development agenda who will carry on the process ahead and without their active participation this cannot be worked out. Because any policy framed by adults overlook children's problem even if they are affected directly or indirectly. Social development planning would remain unsustainable and unsuccessful as long as planners keep children invisible.

Development has always been believed to be a 'top down' process where others decide what the target group should have for their own betterment. But overtime this process has nearly failed and every development sector feels that it should be 'bottom up' approach where participation of the beneficiaries are essential for the successful implementation of the project and its sustenance.

PRA (Participatory Rural Appraisal) has been developed as a method to bridge the gap between the policy maker and the beneficiaries. This is a methodology for interacting with villagers, understanding them and learning from them. It involves a set of principles, a process of communication and a menu of methods for seeking villagers' participation in putting forward their points of view about any issue and enabling them do their own analysis with a view to make use of such learning. It initiates a process and sustains it (Mukherjee, 1993).

PRA is essentially a methodology to offset biases of Rural Development Tourism (RDT) and the survey method. It aims at offsetting such biases by being relaxed and not rushing, listening and not lecturing, probing and not speeding indifferently and looking for participation of rural and other weaker sections of rural communities (Chambers, 1992).

Since PRA aims at addressing the unseen and unheard, this could be the best method to understand children. As a part of our group training in PRA wc had an opportunity to visit a village and do some exercises.

Village Description

The village selected for study was Dosra Khurd, tehsil Phagi, district Jaipur. This village is 50 km. away from Jaipur. The area covered in hectares is 200.73 km., number of occupied residential houses are 32 and number of households are 52. Total population of the village is 319, males 161, and females 158. Total population of the age group of 0-6 is 72, boys 38 and girls 34. The villagers settled in this village in 1950 when the land was granted to them under the Bhoodan movement by Government of India. Village has people belonging to three castes—Rajputs, Berwe and Bagdi. They cultivate a variety of crops round the year except for two summer months. There are no road linkages, water is not safe due to the excess quantity of fluoride. They have livestock like cow, goat, etc. Lok Jumbish Parishad started a school in that village in the later part of 1993. They have the school both in the morning and in the evening. In most households both men and women are busy in the field for the whole day.

Objectives

Though we had a number of areas to select and work on during our one day PRA training programme we decided to work with children.

— The main aim was to apply PRA techniques to children related issues.
— Through different exercises (drawing, daily routine and problems analysis) we wanted to know difference in perception that existed between boys and girls.
— In the drawing exercise we wanted to know the gap between their reality and dream.
— Discussion was used to know their daily routine and understand their workload.

Sample Selection

Children both boys and girls were selected as sample for the exercise. Children who were free and willing to cooperate participated. There were twenty boys in the age range of 3 years to 10 years most of them were school-going.

In the girls group there were five girls in the range of 4 years to 12 years. It was not easy to get more girls because they were busy doing evening work and had no time to sit and do the exercises.

Process

We reached the village around noon and found a number of children playing around. There were about 20 boys and no girls. We started with a round of introduction by telling our names and are purpose of the visit—mainly to learn from them, their life styles. So they were excited to know that elders were there to learn from them and were ready to share everything. They introduced themselves one by one and sat in a circle on a mud floor. Since only boys were available we did some PRA exercises with them (mentioned in this paper). Rapport establishment was not a very difficult thing with them because they were open and communicative.

We had to wait for the girls. Around sun-set they returned with their livestock. They looked tired and it took a lot of time to establish rapport with them. We interacted with them but there was time constraint. It was about to get dark and they had a lot of things to do for the evening meals. With girls we had to probe a lot. They took long to open up and were inhibited. So the interaction with the girls was not very smooth.

We interacted with children discussing about their daily routine and problems. Drawing was used because that helps to overcome the language barrier for the children. As Piaget (1971) in his particular terminology describes imagery as an active, internalized reconstruction of perception where images function as a form of language in expressing their inner thought, feelings and ideas. Discussing daily routine was the other exercise as this would throw light on their daily activities and the amount of time they allocate to each activity. The other exercise was to discuss their problems which could tell us their perception of issue and causes.

Expression through Drawings

We had big chart papers and sketch pens. We all sat on a mud floor in the open, in a circle and started with a round of introduction just by telling the name. Then we asked them if they were interested to make some drawings as the material required was available or would like to do something else. But they were all eager to make drawings.

We facilitated the process, gave them coloured pens and spread drawing sheet on the floor. Then requested them to draw whatever they liked from their daily life. Initially about eight of them started drawing and later others joined them. Within fifteen minutes the paper was filled with pictures of different shape size and colours.(See Figures 2.1, 2.2 and 2.3). Then we requested them to draw what they would like, wish to have or their dreams. It took another half an hour for them to finish that also.

Throughout they enjoyed using pens of different colours. They were not disturbed while drawing. After they finished we asked each one individually what they had drawn and why. All the drawings were interpreted by them individually in the group.

It took a lot of time to built rapport with the girls' group. They were looking tired. They were too shy and not ready to talk. They had just returned with their livestock from the field and it was time for them to fetch water and start cooking evening meals. So their mind was preoccupied with the work load.

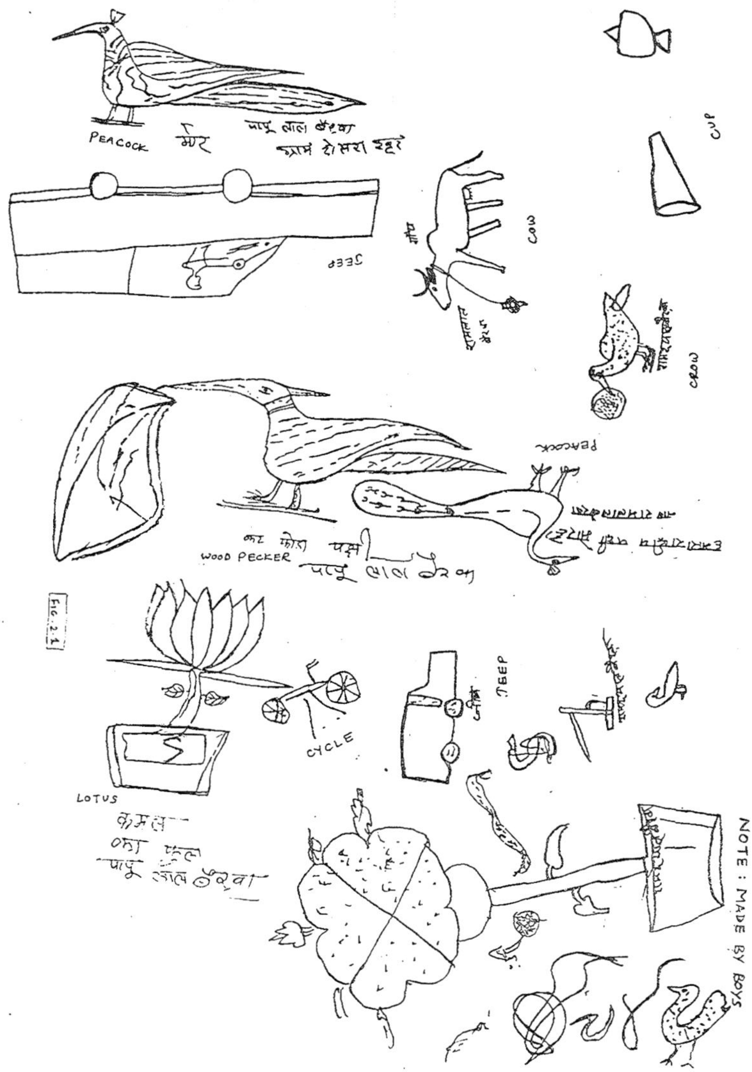
PEACOCK
JEEP
COW
CUP
CROW
PEACOCK
WOOD PECKER
CYCLE
JEEP
LOTUS
NOTE : MADE BY BOYS

FIG. 2.1

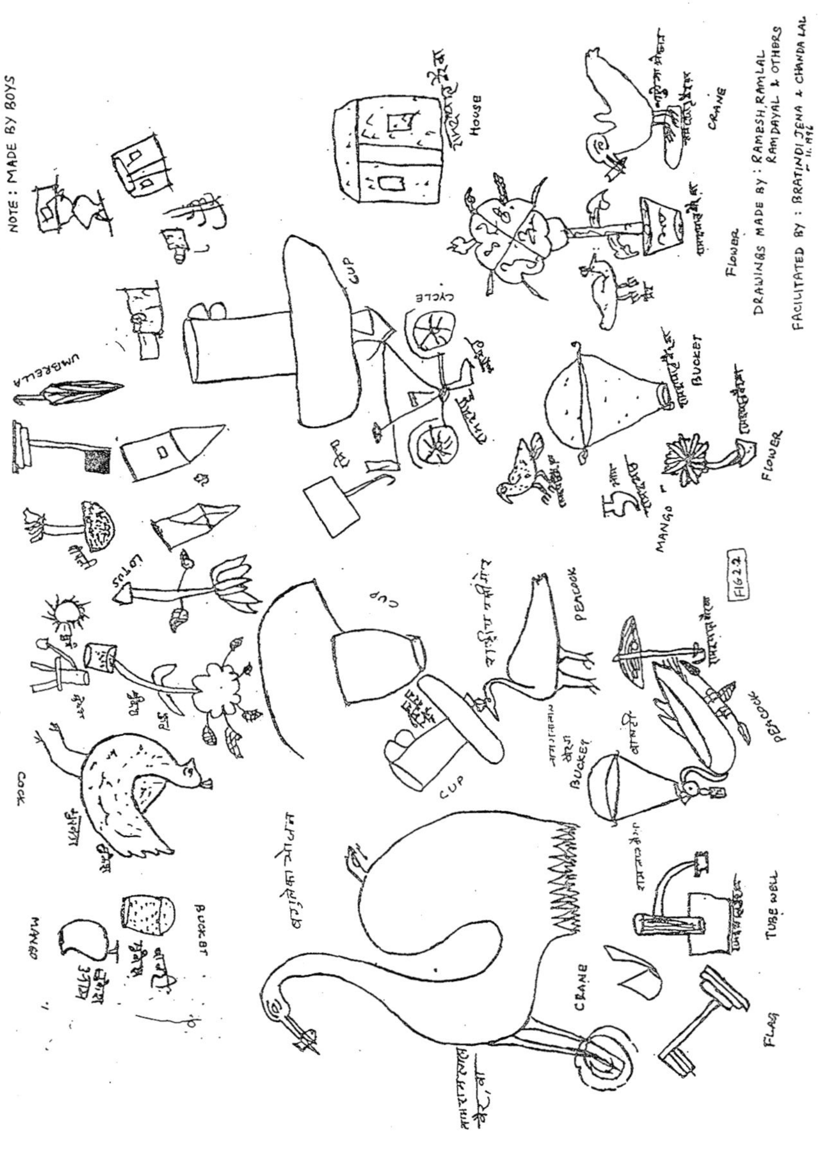
NOTE : MADE BY BOYS
DRAWINGS MADE BY : RAMESH, RAMLAL, RAMDAYAL & OTHERS
FACILITATED BY : BRATINDI JENA & CHANDA LAL
FIG 2.2
HOUSE
CRANE
FLOWER
BUCKET
CUP
CYCLE
UMBRELLA
LOTUS
MANGO
PEACOCK
COCK
TUBE WELL
FLAG

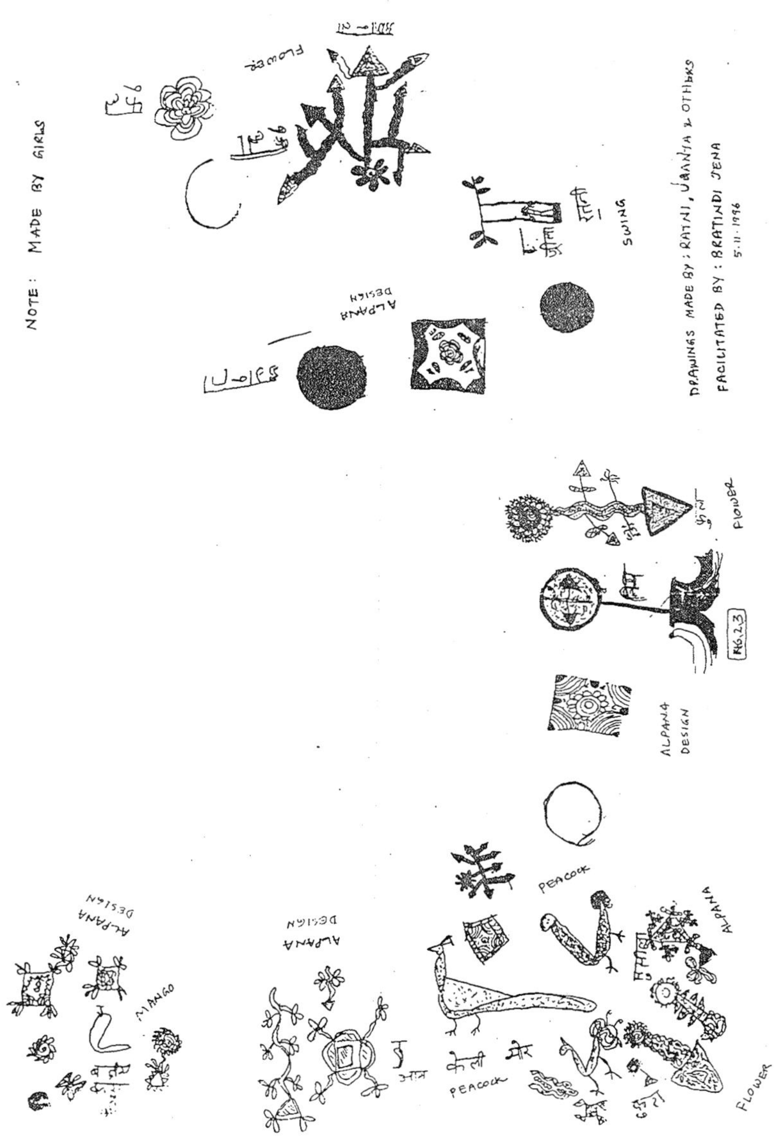
NOTE: MADE BY GIRLS
DRAWINGS MADE BY: RATNI, JAANIA & OTHERS
FACILITATED BY: BRATINDI JENA
5.11.1996
FIG. 2.3
FLOWER
SWING
ALPANA DESIGN
PEACOCK
MANGO
ALPANA

Since very few girls, about five were there we thought of playing some game to break the ice and involve them. But they had no concept of play. "We only work, we have no time to play" was their reply. Then we decided to facilitate the drawing part. Because they really had not much time to spare and it was about to get dark. With a lot of persuasion they started drawing those objects related to their life style. Once they finished with that we requested them to draw their dreams and wishes. We had to help them understand this clearly. It took them quite some time to complete it.

Observations and Interpretation

Boys had very little or no inhibition. They appeared enthusiastic to draw. If it was possible they would have finished all the papers available. But girls on the other hand were too inhibited to hold the pens. They took more time than boys to start. This reflects the difference in social conditioning of both boys and girls. Boys are conditioned to be outgoing extrovert and open where as girls are conditioned to be shy, introvert, to remain indoor. They are not expected to be outgoing, open and communicate with others.

Both the groups were given paper of same size. Boys' drawings were big in size with free hand movement and occupied a fair amount of space on the paper. In fact they filled up the paper. Whereas girls' drawings were small in size, hand movement was restricted and more than half space on the paper remained empty. Boys' drawings were not very close to the edge of the paper but girls' drawings were close to the edge of the paper and rarely moved towards the centre. This reflects the amount of social space each group occupies and their freedom of movement.

The child's drawing become a form of language—a way of expressing concepts and ideas. It is thus a form of calligraphy, a kind of stylized writing. Harris (1963). Boys' drawings were relatively straight, clear and less colourful but girls' drawings were more intricate and colourful. This could be reflecting the feeling of both boys and girls. Boys are conditioned to be less artistic than girls.

Boys drawings were more related to social problems, financial need and comforts of life. Their drawings included items of daily use as well. On the other hand girls' drawings reflected artistic sense. Boys drew cups, bucket, etc. But girls drew "alpana" (design) that they usually put on the door step on festivals. Boys and girls drew one common thing, peacock. Boys drew peacock because they sold beautiful feather and purchased eatables. But girls drew peacock because they liked its voice.

Paivio (1971) remarked that children's drawing is an indication of the development of imaginary or representational thought process. That could be the main reason for girls drawing few items. In fact they could express themselves better in words than in pictures. In their wishes or dreams also boys and girls differed. Boys wanted to have vehicles to increase their mobility. Education was not really important for them, they wanted to acquire more land and livestock and wanted to have tractors. Their main focus was to improve their life style so they focussed on economic items. Girls could not think of any wish or dream. They kept looking at each other and wondered what could be a dream or wish in life because on that issue most of them could not draw anything.

This reflects a deprived state of a women in our society. From childhood she understands that she can't even dream of owning a house, land, livestock which could enhance her condition. No way she can think of improving her life style. Because she is conditioned to be a giver not a taker. The girls could think of a garden with flowers and a swing. They all wanted to study. When I enquired the reason they replied 'we want to teach others'. This reminded me of Mahatma Gandhi's words—"Educate a man, educate an individual, educate a woman, educate a nation".

While discussing their daily routine we came to know that boys had more time for study. In fact they did not have to do much work at home and got full support from the family. On the other hand girls had no time to study. They had to attend the evening school after a hectic day. Very often they found it difficult to understand the lessons because of physical and mental exhaustion. They did not get any support from the family. But they were more interested in studies than boys.

Daily Routine

We discussed the daily routine of both boys and girls to understand division of labour between sexes within the household, time available to study, play and rest.

Boys' Daily Routine

Morning they get up, wash their face, take tea and start playing around for some time and then go to the school. After school take their meals again play around and after evening meals go off to sleep. This is the daily routine of boys who don't look after livestock regularly (see Table 2.1). But the daily routine for boys who have to look after livestock is different and their number is less (see Table 2.2). Only two boys are doing this regularly. After tea they play around till the animals are ready to be taken out. They take their lunch packs with them and return in the evening. They attend evening school and go off to sleep after evening meals.

TABLE 2.1: Normal Daily Routine Activities of Male Child

Washing face	—	early morning
Drinking tea	—	morning
Play activities		
School		
After coming back from school they again go for		
—	play	
—	have food (dinner)	
—	go to bed.	

TABLE 2.2: The Daily Routine Activities and Activities of a Herder Male Child

—	taking animals for grazing to fallow lands
—	play activities in the afternoon
—	have dinner
—	go to bed.

Girls' Daily Routine

The daily routine of girls was somewhat different (Table 2.3). Their day starts early in the morning, they make tea for every one, clean the house, courtyard, fetch water, cook food for the day, give fodder to livestock. Around noon they go to the field with the livestock. During that period they are engaged in other activities like harvesting crop, collecting fuel, fodder, picking up groundnut, etc. In the evening, they return back to the village. Again fill water, cook evening meals and go to school. After school they take their evening meals and go off to sleep. This was only a rough sketch of their daily routine. Apart from these, activities looking after old grand-parents, ailing elders and younger children are also included in their daily routine. This depends upon the number of dependents the family has. The girls daily routine was really an unbelievable fact. But we could find few studies supporting their daily routine.

TABLE 2.3: The Daily Routine Activities of the Girl Child

Morning activities
Washing face
Tea preparation
Cleaning the house
Cleaning the cattleshed
Preparing the lunch
Afternoon activities
Working in the forests
Filling water
Harvesting
Evening activities
Preparing dinner
Going to evening school
Going to bed

A study conducted by UNICEF (1990) reveals that younger children work longer hours than the older children. In Rajasthan, the girls worked longer than boys. Girls from Rajasthan worked not only longer than boys but were involved in all agricultural activities, except ploughing and irrigation. Work participation data of same study indicates that in the age group of 9 to 14 years old, rural girl spends on an average 8 hours on production and domestic work which is 3 hours more than that of boys. Female children substitute for female adults in many of their roles and so have less access to the social infrastructure especially education (Jain 1980).

Children's Problem

Boys

Boys were quite enthusiastic to vent their problems. They started mentioning their problems one after the other without any inhibition. 'No money' was their first problem followed by lack of proper teaching, unclean school environment, lack of play ground and drinking water. They went into detail discussion on each problem. Their purchasing capacity was limited due to lack of money. They had a lot of free time to play but no play grounds. After putting the problems or issues on paper I asked them to do the scoring, e.g., give maximum scores to the problem they felt was acute and minimum to the one which they considered to be least important. They were free to score in their own way but decided to put scores between 1 to 10 (Table 2.4). After they scored the problems we rechecked the scores with them and they were satisfied.

TABLE 2.4: Problems of Boys with Searing and Ranking by them

Boys Problems	Scores	Ranks
No Money	9	2
Teaching	7	4
Unclean school environment	10	1
No play ground	6	5
Drinking water	8	3

TABLE 2.5: Problems of Girls with Scoring and Ranking by Them

Girls problems	Scores	Ranks
No time to rest	6	5
Get tired easily	7	4
A lot of field work	10	1
Looking after livestock	9	2
Attending school at night	5	6
Cooking	8	3

Girls

Discussing problems with the girls was an uphill task. For some time there was complete silence and then came the reply "we are all happy, we have no problems 'no difficulties'. Most probably they failed to perceive their own difficulties and to express the same due to socio cultural conditioning.

As Cross and Baker puts it women tend to reflect less critically on their life situation, attributing their hardships to fate rather than external factors! This often makes it more difficult for the interviewer to follow up further lines of questioning.

While accepting openly that they were right in their perception. We started probing indirectly to know what was most difficult for them in the daily household chores. Then we moved on to drinking water and evening school issues. Within few minutes they started talking about the drudgery of field work followed by looking after livestock, cooking, feeling exhausted, lack of rest and school at night (Table 2.5). They talked about each issue, the details and mentioned that was the reason they had no time to play.

Here, there is a clear difference in the perception of problem of both the sexes and in expressing it, though they live in the same village under almost similar conditions.

Boys were more vocal and their problems were related to outdoor activities. Money was meaningful for them because they had power to access it. They were not happy with the teacher because they had opportunity to avail money. Girls on the other hand had no vision of money. They were conditioned to be happy with whatever they had. School in the evening was a boon to them, so they had no complaints about the teaching or the unclean environment. Girls felt inhibited in expressing their problem because they are brought up in a 'silent culture' they are expected to be tolerant and accept of every hardship. Their difficulties were related to their daily activity. They had no concept of a play ground because they have no time to play.

Memorable Event

By the time we finished talking to the girls it was about to get dark. So we were in a hurry to wind up everything. Within half an hour. we were near our jeeps to leave the village. Suddenly we noticed one girl looking at us from a distance. She was the first girl we met when their group came with the goats and cows. She helped us call all her friends to one place. We went to say good-bye, she looked so different to us all of a sudden. In her expression she had 'a lot to say'. But still an invisible heavy curtain was around her. She asked 'when will you come again?' We really don't know was our reply. She was silent after that and our driver was desperate to start. So to comfort her we said 'hopefully we meet again' and smiled at her but she had a cold expression on her face and we had to move to the vehicle. Her hand was held to convey that we understood what she wanted to say and walked with her to the jeep. When the jeep started we waved at each other.

She was about seven years old. While discussing about the difficulties she kept saying I am happy I have no problem throughout even when everyone else started talking about their difficulties. She never changed her words. Throughout she was smiling. She took a lot of time to start the drawing and made few small things and stopped.

On our way back we kept thinking about her what she might be wanting to tell. May be she is passing through a very oppressed childhood and needed more time and a safe space to reveal herself . Most probably she was not comfortable in the group and needed individual attention.

We all carry a preconceived notion about children that they have no inhibitions about their expressions. Is that same for a girl child also, where she loses her childhood even before she is five years old and carries around a lot of household responsibilities. We shall never forget her pair of eyes filled with a desire to reveal something confidently. Each time while talking to a group of girls we must remember that someone might need little more time and space than others.

Strengths of the Study

We reached village around noon when most adults were in the fields and only children were playing. So we did not have much of a problem in gathering children. Since parents were not around children had full freedom to express themselves. There was no interference from elders. Drawing as the first exercise helped in facilitating the rapport building process for both the teams that really helped in opening up. For the first time we could know about the store of knowledge children have and its value.

The most invisible and unheard section of the society was studied here. We could get a clear picture of their own perception. Socialization and conditioning from childhood was crystal clear. Gender biases were also reflected upon. For creating a healthy and harmonious society gender gap could be addressed from childhood.

This has thrown light on certain myths related to childhood, e.g., that they are ignorant, have no inhibitions and they understand nothing, etc.

We think children are more sensitive than adults. They have their own vision of the world that does not match an adult and is rejected as inappropriate. Because no one takes the pain to understand them. There was no language barrier in this exercise, we could understand each other well.

Limitations

Time constraint was the biggest limitation of this study. We needed more time with the girls group. We could have given more time and space to them to express. We could cover only three phases of exercise. If time permitted I could have done few more for further interaction like story telling, free association, etc. We could have gone for a joint walk to know how much knowledge they have about their own village.

Outcome

Reaching out to children is not difficult. If one has the willingness and patience it can be done easily. Children's ways of communication is clear. They can express a lot through a small drawing which might not hold any meaning for an adult. Their difficulties should be looked at from their perspective. What they find difficult at their age must be having some physical and psychological implications and must not be neglected. The gender difference that exists in the society right from childhood is clearly visible in all three exercises. This could grow with them and continue unless corrected on time. Childhood is the phase where one has maximum chance to build one's image and self-concept. So behaviour pattern could be studied to improve upon their future.

Implications

With the help of such studies existing gender discrimination could be addressed so that the gap is bridged at the right time. It would help children develop a positive self-concept and make them confident. They will learn to value themselves. A clear vision of their difficulties can help policy makers and NGOs to identify the area of attention. Children's perceptions at the local level can help the village, panchayat frame schemes to benefit them directly.

Acknowledgement

The author wishes to thank all the children of the village Dosra Khurd who spare their valuable time. The author is also grateful to Dr. Neela Mukherjee for encouraging her to write this paper. She thanks Dr. Pradeep Bhargav and all her colleagues at IDS, Jaipur for their kind cooperation.

REFERENCES

Chambers, Robert (1992), *Rural Appraisal: Rapid, Relaxed and Participatory, Discussion,* Paper No. 311, Institute of Development Studies, Sussex, October.

Cross, N. and R. Baker, *At the Desert's Edge: Oral Histories from the Sahel,* Panos/SOS Sahel.

Deshpande, Avinash (1996), *Towards a Children's Agenda: New Challenges for Social Development,* SAC.

Harris, D.B., (1963) *Children's Drawings as Measures of Intellectual Maturity,* Harcourt, Brace and World.

Jain, Devaki (1980), *Women's Employment as Related to Rural Areas—India.* World Conference of United Nations: Mid-decade for Women, Copenhagen, Denmark.

Mukherjee, Neela (1993), *Participatory Rural Appraisal: Methodology and Application*—Concept.

Paivio, A., (1971), *Imagery and Verbal Processes,* Holt, Rinehart and Winston, New York.

Piaget, J., (1971), Inhelder, B. *et al.,* Mental Imagery in the Child, Routledge and Kegan Paul.

UNICEF (1990), *Children and Women in India—A Situational Analysis,* New Delhi, pp. 78-79.

3

PARTICIPATORY TEACHING
Learning Process in Primary Education

— MEERA JAYASWAL

In this paper participatory teaching-learning process (PTLP) was applied on an exploratory basis to children of primary schools in villages of Bero situated in Ranchi District of Bihar. Such a process was applied to examine its impact on primary school children in improving their level of educational attainment in language and mathematics. This was to be compared with the conventional teaching-learning process where the students were recipient of unilateral teacher's instructions. PTLP was based on children's experience, familiar activities, objects, stories, games and songs. The results show that such PTLP not only led to better educational attainments in language and mathematics but also improved the class room culture.

Conventional Teaching-Learning Process and Children's Educational Attainment

The conventional teaching-learning process follows 'top-down' model based on teacher's teaching module prepared by so called "experts" of "apex" organization. The teaching aids and examples are taken from metropolis and thus neglecting the indigenous experience to which children are exposed. The teachers cover syllabus by dictating notes. The children are required to undergo rote learning process by recalling foreign words and examples. Mugging up answers to expected questions are very common. Such teaching-learning process impairs the functioning of children, both individually and in their social capacity which can be termed as pathological (Chowdhury, 1994). Reimer (1972) believes that the school is dead because its formalism discourages innovation and individual responses.

As a result of the prevailing teaching-learning process the level of academic attainment in children has become low not only in states like Bihar with low literacy but also in state like Kerala with high literacy.

In Mallapuram district of Kerala, more than 45 per cent of the children completing primary education could not write five Malyalam words correctly. In Maharashtra, Maxine Bernstein found that more than 50 per cent of grade II children had not mastered the skills appropriate for grade I. Neerja Sharma carried out a study on class V grade children in Agra and Lucknow districts of Uttar Pradesh. She found that a mastery level performance was achieved by slightly over two per cent of the children in Hindi, less than one per cent in environmental study and less than six per cent in arithmetic (Kumar, 1994).

In a baseline study, conducted by National Council of Educational Research and Training in 1992-93, the following facts were outlined : (1) Among Class V students, the maximum students achieved 20 out of 40 in word meaning (50 per cent) and 17 out of 44 in reading comprehension (39 per cent), (2) Among class IV students, even in Kerala, the maximum score on word comprehension was 58 per cent and in reading comprehension it was 56 percent. (3) In reading comprehension, no district in Madhya Pradesh and Tamil Nadu achieved an average score of 40 per cent, (4) Learning achievements in mathematics were even lower than in reading. The maximum student achievement score in class IV and V in any of the State was 48 per cent. More than 80 per cent of the students reading in class IV or V in Assam, Haryana, Kerala, Maharashtra, Madhya Pradesh and Orissa could not achieve a minimum score of 40 per cent (UNICEF, 1995).

Sample Design for the Study

The study was carried out in six schools[1] which were selected from six villages in rural areas of Bero in Ranchi, Bihar. Of the six schools PTLP was applied to four of them and conventional teaching-learning process was applied to the rest.[2] A total of 405 children enrolled in class I of the schools constituted the sample of the study.

Tools Used

The following tools were used in this study.

— Educational Attainment Test (EAT) of language and mathematics was used to measure the level of educational attainment of children. The items of the test was based on competencies of language and mathematics (NCERT: 1991). The items of EAT were prepared by participatory exercise of primary school teachers, research investigators and educational psychologists. A pilot test was also done on 30 children of two schools selected from villages of Bero.

— Focus Group Discussions with teachers and parents were undertaken to know about the existing teaching-learning process of those sample schools.

Teachers' Perceptions

On asking the teachers the following problems were highlighted—

(i) They wanted to finish the syllabus
(ii) Very few teaching aids were used
(iii) Teaching aids were not prepared in schools
(iv) Children were not encouraged for child to child learning
(v) Rapport was not smooth between teachers and children
(vi) All children were not involved in school activities
(vii) The no-cost and low-cost local resources were not utilised in schools
(viii) Children were not encouraged to "speak" and "read" neither were they exposed to extra classroom environment.

What emerges out of the discussion that teaching was one sided, it was teacher-oriented rather than learner-oriented. The 'rote memory' was evaluated leaving "understanding" on the side track.

Parents' Perceptions

Most of the parents believed that children did not have interest in school education. Parents were ambivalent about the teaching-learning process. They said that they did not have time to interact with teachers. Most of the children did not study at home at all. Parents had negative attitude towards education because it had nothing to do with solving everyday life problems.

Discussion with Children, Parents and Teachers

The content of PTLP was prepared on the basis of discussion with newly enrolled Class I children. A list of their experiences, activities, familiar objects, known stories and songs was prepared. Discussions were also held with parents and teachers to explore further and also validate such list.

The responses of participants were summed up and categorised as follows.

(a) Activities

— Visiting market with elders including parents, siblings and other relatives.
— Visiting agricultural fields with parents.
— Visiting fields with elder sibling for grazing animals.
— Doing light household work, such as room cleaning, carrying water from hand pump or well in small container, plucking vegetables.
— Playing local games.

(b) Material and Objects

Animals and birds such as cow, ox, goat, pig, dog, duck, hen, sparrow, crow, pigeon, horse etc.

(c) Trees and Plants

Mango, guava, jackfruit, custard apple (sarifa), rose apple, tamarind etc.

(d) Utensils

Plate (thali), glass, bucket, mug, bowl etc.

(e) Fruits and Vegetables

Mango, guava, jackfruit, custard apple (sarifa), tamarind, forum, banana, potato, tomato, onion, bottle gourd, cauliflower, carrot, raddish, groundnut, mulberry.

(f) Collection of familiar songs, stories and games

Implementation of Participatory Teaching-Learning Process

(i) The first few days of children in school were exercised as 'revision period'. The teacher was facilitator. He made each child to narrate his experience of 'agricultural field', 'market', 'grazing field' or any other such experiences that they had. He requested them to perform very simple activity that they had already performed, they were asked to play that had already been played. The teacher encouraged children to speak about fruits, vegetables trees and plants that they knew.
This revision period was supposed to break the ice, to establish a cordial rapport between teacher and children.

(ii) The teacher, then proceeded to play. If masks were available, children and teachers mimicked the actions of masks that they were wearing, and sound of mask-animal or birds. In course of play, simple question-answer exercises were practiced by asking simple questions such as. 'Have you seen a goat?, 'Do you have goat in your house ? etc.

(iii) The teacher proceeded to 'story telling-listening process'. He asked as to how many children had heard any story ? If it appeared that children were aware of stories, he requested them to tell them. He observed all children and involved them by asking simple questions and also minutely observed their gestures. This practice led to initiate children's habit listening with understanding to simple, familiar and popular stories, poems and tales.
If children did not respond of their awareness about tales or stories, the teacher told very short humerous tale or story and involved all children for the development of children's listening habit.
The teacher made learning climate more lively by 'role playing' and holding conversation between various actions. These strengthened children's ability to 'understand conversation and dialogues in familiar situation and 'respond to oral instructions in familiar; situation and 'to repeat simple sentences correctly'.

(iv) Teacher requested the children to sing any song that they were knowing. He added gestures associated with lines of song. This activity helped children to establish an association between language and activities leading to make the language more meaningful and easy.

(v) For counting, visible trees, animals or children were used. The mathematical concepts were taught first with the help of objects and pictures and after that they were introduced to writing stage.

Teachers considered the following points while interacting with children and parents :

— Respecting each and every child and calling every child by his/her full name.
— Listening to childrens experiences, stories, songs, narration and discussion.
— Using local, clear and simple language, teaching aids and materials that every one could understand.
— Participating in games and activities with children.
— Praising children for good behaviour.
— Involving children in the preparation of teaching-aids for themselves.
— Quoting examples from familiar experiences, situations and events.
— Visiting children's houses and giving suggestions in a friendly way.
— Organising parent-teacher meetings.
— Inviting parents, particularly mothers for story telling, singing, role playing and similar such activities.

Achievements

The impact of PTLP was shown by comparing the following observations in educational attainments of children and classroom atmosphere.

Improved Educational Attainment

The mean scores of children increased from 67.91 to 90.45 in experimental schools and from 68.92 to 70.55 in controlled schools.

The full marks were 200.

Due to PTLP, the percentage of children reduced from lower level of educational attainment (achieving less than 40 per cent score) and increased in higher levels of achievements (achieving more than 40 per cent score) in language as well as mathematics. This kind of a trend was observed in controlled schools.

Classroom Atmosphere

The following observations regarding classroom atmosphere of experimental and controlled schools were made by research investigators, co-investigators and principal investigators.

Experimental Schools	*Control Schools*
Teaching Aids	
Plenty of teaching-aids were prepared by local, low-cost or no-cost resources and used extensively by teachers as well as students.	Very few or no teaching-aids were available, the teaching was based on text books only.
Rapport	
Rapport between teachers and Children were warm and cordial with almost all children.	Warm and cordial behaviour were limited to very few selected children.
Behaviour of Children	
Responsive, answered spontaneously to the questions asked.	Passive and silent to the questions asked
Class-room Atmosphere	
Lively, children were relaxed, active, enthusiastic.	Dull, tense, reluctant yawning, and sleeping.

Underlying Factors related to Achievement

- Teaching-learning in PTLP became two-way, Children were not receipient of teachers' instructions rather they also participated actively.
- Rapport between teacher and children created a warm and cordial atmosphere. Children were in a position to express their knowledge freely without any inhibitions.
- Children's experiences were fully recognized and were integrated in PTLP. This enhanced their self-esteem and thereby had a positive impact on their need for achievement.
- A discussion with parents helped teachers to understand children's capabilites and skills which led to need assessment of threshold level for PTLP.
- Child-to-child learning was encouraged in story-telling, role playing, games and songs. Thus learning became enjoyable and creative.

The present study is an exploratory one based on small homogeneous sample for which the results in terms of childrens's achievement in primary school through PTLP is encouraging and such exploratory studies are required to be undertaken with larger samples so as to arrive at a set of results which can have significant implications for policy-making related to universalization of primary education. Such participatory approach to teaching-learning can help in reducing the proportion of school drop-outs, make education innovative and realistic and also help in compensating the acute lack of schooling infrastructure in state-run schools.

Acknowledgements

I am grateful to all individuals and institutions who facilitated for the preparation of this paper. The experience and data of the paper is based on MLL Project of Ranchi University. Dr. A. Hans, Dr. Anujee Choudhary, Dr. Anita Arora, Dr. N.K. Tah, Farzana Bano, Anita Prasad, Children, parents and teachers of Bero block, helped in a very positive and smooth way during the implementation of the project. Prof. A. K. Singh provided guidance in various stage of the work.

NOTES

1. Experiment Schools (ES): Jaria Middle School, Haria; Kuli Middle school, Kuli; Tengaria Primary School Tengaria; Bhendra Primary School, Bhendra.
2. Controlled Schools (CS): Katarmali Primary School, Katarmali, Govt. Girls Middle School, Bero.

REFERENCES

Chaudhary, J.C. (1994). The Pathology of Learning. *Indian Educational Review,* 29, 82-88.

Kumar, K. (1994). Primary Failure. *Future: Development Perspectives on Children,* 31-32, 5.

NCERT (1991). *Minimum Levels of Learning at Primary Stage.* NCERT: New Delhi.

Reimer, E. (1972). *The School is Dead.* Harmondsworth : Penguin

UNICEF (1995). *The Progress of States 1995,* p 50. New Delhi : UNICEF.

GENDER EMPOWERMENT
Learning from Women

4

HIDDEN AGENDA

— INDIRA KOHLI

A village lives at many levels, the uppermost, superficial one being transparent to all. Here, communication is through the menfolk, the absence or degree of interaction by the women being directly proportional to the isolation or distance from the nearest town and external contact.

The depth to which one can delve into village life depends on frequency of contact and persistent, consistent, yet gentle confidence building measures and participation in the social life of the village. Here, conscious direction is given towards merging, ultimately evolving to acceptance.

The second, the economic level constitutes the foundation of village life, and initially all participatory programmes will silently revolve around the degree of ultimate economic advantage that will accrue to each family.

Much can be learned through participatory methods of rural appraisal which encourage the villagers to voice their visions for the future of their village and to enunciate their own needs. The motivator is mainly a silent observer during meetings, motivating the villagers towards rooted, participatory economic and ecologically sustainable growth. The motivator also encourages sharing and the uniform spreading of economic benefits that can be earned through projects, particularly the labour intensive. But there is a deeper, sometimes darker level.

For the village to achieve success this level must be plumbed, recognised, understood and handled with caution through this understanding.

The village is beautiful. The uppermost hamlet spreads across a level surface towards the top of the spur. The soil is loamy, and the fields well irrigated by cemented channels that direct the waters of the abundantly flowing springs located in the forest above the village which is populated by upper-caste families. A wide but rough path leads down to the second hamlet populated by lower caste families. The dwellings hug the hill slope following the contours of its curves. Small huts, small land holdings.

The third hamlet nestles in a basin at the base of the slope. It is dissected by a stream that has carved its bed deeper and ever deeper, its depth now such that it can no longer irrigate the fields. A footpath winding through a forest forms the approach to this hamlet populated by scheduled caste families.

On her first day at the village the motivator trudged towards the village tap. Greeting the two women who were chatting while washing their clothes, she entered into conversation, and then asked if she could have a drink of water. "Water? No, no" exclaimed one. "Come and I will make for you some tea, you are our guest. No, don't worry, you are not disturbing us we have finished our work here". So saying, the two women quickly spread the washed clothes along a wire fence and led her to their houses adjacent to each other. By the end of the tea session the motivator had made two friends and some acquaintances. By the end of two weeks, the village women were looking out for her arrival, usually in the afternoon.

The women had worked out an activity circle in a game on the earthen floor of a courtyard. The findings had shown the motivator that at this time of day they were free of chores.

Gradually, the women began to congregate on the verandah of the Panchayat building and the PRA process was initiated. Prior to entry into the village, the motivator had studied the Block records, the maps pertaining to the area and she had done her homework well. She waited for the group to mention the presence of the other two hamlets but they were silent.

One afternoon, the women prioritized their needs, the first being a cutting and tailoring course. The motivator knew it was now high time to initiate the entry of the other two hamlets.

"Are there no other hamlets ?"
"Well yes, two "
"Let us go and visit them"
"They are far"

"Well then, let us call them here. Perhaps they too may like to learn cutting and tailoring"

"There is not enough room"

"They can sit on the verandah or we can spread a dhurrie in the courtyard"

"Hm-m, we could"

And so they did.

The tailoring classes were well attended and the motivator, having a fair idea of average income levels through PRA probing, managed to collect old saries as materials for stitching for the women of hamlets two and three who sat on the dhurrie in the courtyard.

One cloudy afternoon rain began to pelt down and the motivator rushed the women on to the verandah. Their dhurrie was laid out neatly, and they completed their lesson. Thereafter they quietly continued their classes on the verandah. One of the scheduled caste women was an excellent student and soon she was helping the cutting and tailoring teacher within the class room itself.

One day two visitors came to the village during the sewing period and they bought and paid for two baby frocks and one *petticoat.* Expectations rose sky-high and the women were fired with the ambition of earning money.

Now was the time for the second step thought the social worker. "What will you all do with this money you are going to earn?"

"We'll buy cows and sell the milk"

"But then, how will you feed them?"

"Look at the forest around you! Can't you see the leaves?"

"Oh yes, but when the leaves finish?"

"We'll let some of the water from our irrigation channels flow into the forest to grow more leaves".

"But there will be no water because you will have destroyed the trees and you know that the springs can't live without foliage"

The women became nervous. "Come, let us all walk to the springs".

"The water is less. Look here's the old level!" Urgent discussions were held, and ultimately the village women decided to plant tree saplings of their choice.

"Do you think it would be a good idea to dig out the "lantana"

weeds first?"
"Oh impossible, they are too thorny!"
"What a pity, I had managed to get an Agency to pay you all for the work"
"Not all "lantana" is thorny. How much?"
"Government rates".
What? It's too little. We must be paid more. Look at the thorns! Look at the roots!"
Government rates".

Ultimately, the motivator picked up a pick-axe and commenced digging out the "lantana" herself. Enthusiasm soon raged and work commenced. They cleaned the area, planted fuel and fodder saplings of their choice. They even worked out a system for social fencing through fines on owners of trespassing livestock, and the women were each responsible for an equal number of trees!

When payments were made, the upper caste women thanked her but commented on low government rates. The women from the second and third hamlets were ecstatic. They immediately walked with greater confidence, and arrived at the sewing class wearing cheap but new saris.

The motivator next explained the advantages of forming a revolving fund and urged the women to think of pooling some of the money earned. A fund was soon instituted but for the women of only the upper-most hamlet. Bonding, participation, were still inadequate but the motivator was confident that these would soon evolve. All must be participatively involved for village growth to be sustainable.

The motivator encouraged joint activities thus aiding the formation of inter-hamlet bonds; the first activity was a highly successful health camp, then a children's competition.

Soon it was time to commence planting on a very large "lantana" infested hill slope. The topic was broached one afternoon and the motivator, in fact all the women present felt uneasy at the total lack of enthusiasm shown by a few of the women of the upper-most hamlet. The motivator had remembered the violent reaction to "lantana" eradication work on the first plot, so she had earlier discussed the new work area with a few of the women from the uppermost hamlet enlisting their support at the meeting. No support was forthcoming. So she waited. A few sewing classes later she casually tossed in the subject of the new project, but the women looked at each other in silence. About a week later one of the women whispered to her that the area was a burial ground for children born dead. "Oh no!" She gasped in sadness "No one mentioned it when we surveyed the hill, not even the Headman".

The motivator walked to the slope. "No, it's got to be done. The entire hill will soon be eroded if we don't act now. We can fence off that area". She called a meeting of the women, put forward the idea of fencing, and begged them to think of a future without water, no fuel, no fodder. "What is the good of learning a skill to earn money when the existence of your village and fields has no future". "No" whispered a young woman "If we touch their soil they will come to haunt us, isn't that so elder sister?" she asked one of the motivator's staunch supporters. The woman shuddered, covered her head and looked down. The meeting closed. Everyone dispersed quietly. That night the social worker lay awake for a long time. Was the uneasiness arising from the spirits of dead babes? Was it an exchange of looks that she could not quite fathom? Was it over-tiredness?

Next morning, she threw the entire project out of her mind and commenced work on helping the women organise a Sports Day which they had requested for after having witnessed such an event at their Primary School.

One evening before leaving the village the motivator wandered around to the back of the hill where she had hoped a forest would grow to bless the village with its bounty. Two women from the uppermost hamlet came running after her, and with repeated pleas for her safety would let her go no further. The trio walked back. The motivator wished them and walked down to the second hamlet. She well knew that if a community is to prosper, their suggestions, their wants must be expressed by them.

Nevertheless she said, "you have no water for your fields". The die was cast and she held her breath in anxiety at having even planted the germ of a want in their heads.

"Oh yes, there is always the rain".
"The cement channels can't be built down to our hamlet"
"Who said?"
"We were told".

The motivator turned to some women from the third hamlet, also a scheduled caste group "And you? You have water". She stated.

One of the young women sighed, "I hear the stream all the time. One night when my child was ill and our store of water was finished I went down, down, right down the path with a bucket to fetch some of the cool water with which to bathe my child's head. I was so sad to see so much water but none for us that I even prayed God to let the stream flow upward". The women laughed, but the motivator said, "Water can flow upward. Have you heard of a pump or a hydram?"

"Oh yes, our men spoke about this but they don't agree. "Who, don't agree?" asked the motivator gently, realising she was treading on delicate ground. "They" said another in a tone of dispair pointing to the uppermost hamlet of upper caste families.

As she walked home the motivator wondered how the two women from the upper most hamlet had dared to walk after her on the now 'haunted' hill slope, and felt that perhaps her pleas were now being heard.

The next morning she again deliberately walked to the hill slope hoping to be able to perhaps get the women to now fence off some of the area.

"Here, pass me the rope, this "lantana" is really strongly rooted" called one woman.
"I'll help"
"We should better get back home now".
"This evening, at what time?"
"A little later than yesterday, someone was watching me".

The motivator stood too stunned to utter a word. Then one of the women saw her and called out to the others to come and greet her.

"But how? When? What happened? When did you all start work on this slope ?" Asked the motivator.
"Everyone else was frightened so we decided to take it up", said one.
"But there are only seven of you?"
"Well, we were the ones who were ready to work here".

The motivator looked from one face to another, to another. "Did you tell the others you were starting work?" She asked "If they had wanted to work they could have come, you made no boundary to your offer" said another.

"Ah well", smiled the motivator "I am so glad you have started the work, you are very good, brave woman. Of course, you can now invite the others in, it's not too late, and they will follow your bravery".

The seven women looked at each other in horror. There was dead silence, even the wind stilled its sigh. At last, the leader spoke, "But we've done all the work we've pulled out the "lantana".

"Then share out the digging of holes and planting" suggested the motivator.
"No, no, they won't agree!"
"It will be a confusion!"
"They'll fight about the money!"
"We'll each get less trees, ... no, no, not less trees, its nothing. They just won't agree".

"The village may give us a party", said the leader "we have saved the spring waters". "Yes" said the motivator and congratulated them heartily.
A few days later the motivator went to visit the leader of the planting group.

"It was you who initially said it was a burial ground for children, wasn't it?"
"Hm-m-m, this grinding of masala always stings my eyes. What did you say?"
"You heard".
"Oh, the burial ground! I don't remember, was it me?"
"Yes, it was. Where did you hear this story?"
"Story? shh-sh-h. Don't make jokes, who knows if their spirits will suddenly pounce on us".
"My dear sister. Just tell me one thing. Why did you spread such a story?"
"What else would have stopped them?"
"Oh no! You mean you really wanted to stop them from participating in this project, the project you all prepared together! But why?"
"Well, . . . I don't know. This masala stings my eyes. It's a buirial ground. Aren't you frightened?".
"How have you hidden your work from the other women of this your own hamlet? They must have . . . "

But of course they are also helping, we work in shifts. Please do not think we do not participate of course we do". She thought a moment then added "There is another area on the far side of the village, we'll ask the women of the other two hamlets if they would like to work there. We will all participate. We'll discuss. We'll hold a meeting".

But my dear sister, that area is very small" "Oh, oh yes it is, isn't it" but we can all share. That will be good, won't it?"

That night the motivator made some calculations of area, costs and benefits. At the end of it she gasped aloud "These women will net about five thousand rupees each, plus fuel, and with fodder trees for future milch-cows". They had assessed a resource and had successfully yet ruthlessly schemed to corner it.

The motivator thought of the second and third hamlets. "Poverty alleviation?" She asked herself with tears in her eyes.

5

TRAINING FOR WOMEN'S POLITICAL PARTICIPATION

— MITALI SEN GAVAI

The Seventy third Constitution Amendment Act seeks to initiate a process of rural transformation through popular participation. Women have been envisioned as the principal actors in this process of decentralised development. The Amendment Act has set the stage for gender participation in the Panchayat institutions of local self-governance. The process of gender participation is however, inhibited by the prevalent patriarchal social modes. Also, a majority of the first generation women panchayat functionaries lack the political education and skills required to negotiate the new responsibilities thrust upon them. Capacity building of the women functionaries is therefore, an imperative need for actualising gender participation in the panchayats. The onus for realising the spirit of the Amendment Act thus rests essentially upon the practitioners of development training. The author who herself is a trainer, continuously interacts with a broad spectrum of women functionaries and their trainers in Maharashtra. This paper flows from the experiences that have been articulated by both sets of actors. The paper attempts to identify the nature of the challenges that are confronting training practitioners who are working in this realm of development training.

The Mandate

The Seventy Third Constitution Amendment Act mandates the creation of a separate gender space in the panchayats[1], thus:

Article 243D

(1) Seats shall be reserved for—(a) the Scheduled Castes; and (b) the Scheduled Tribes in every Panchayat and the number of seats so reserved shall bear as nearly as may be, the same proportion to the number of seats to be filled by direct election in that panchayat as the population of the Scheduled Castes in that Panchayat area or of the Scheduled Tribes in that Panchayat area bears to the total population of that area and such seats may be allotted by rotation to different constituencies in a Panchayat.

(2) Not less than one-third of the total number of seats reserved under clause (1) shall be reserved for women belonging to the Scheduled Castes or, as the case may be, the Scheduled Tribes.

(3) Not less than one-third (including the number of seats reserved for women belonging to the Scheduled Castes and the Scheduled Tribes) of the total number of seats to be filled by direct election in every Panchayat shall be reserved for women and such seats may be allotted by rotation to different constituencies in a Panchayat.

(4) The offices of the Chairpersons in the Panchayats at the village or any other level shall be reserved for the Scheduled Castes, the Scheduled Tribes and women in such manner as the Legislature of a State may, by law, provide:

Provided that the number of offices of the Chairpersons reserved for Scheduled Castes and the Scheduled Tribes in the Panchayats at each level in any State shall bear, as nearly as may be, the same proportion of the total number of such offices in the Panchayats at each level as the population of the Scheduled Castes in the State or of the Scheduled Tribes in the State bears to the total population of the State;

Provided further that not less than one-third of the total number of offices of Chairpersons in the Panchayats at each level shall be reserved for women;

Provided also that the number of offices reserved under this clause shall be allotted by rotation to different Panchayats at each level.

The Amendment Act has opened the flood gates of political participation to women at the grassroots. Like all other social institutions, the panchayats have been dominated by strong patriarchal hierarchies that have kept gender participation peripheral within them. This has reinforced the existing inequalities by largely ignoring gender interests in development. The conflict over resources available for development is at the heart of the panchayat political process. This distributional conflict is based upon both socio-economic status and gender. The reservation of one-third seats for women in the panchayats is a device for compelling the resource allocative processes in panchayats to effect redistribution on the side of gender. As women attain increasing control in these institutions, they will challenge and modify the inequities in the process of resource distribution. Thus, the inclusion of gender in the making of development choices is expected to change the very course of development.

The philosophical underpinnings for this policy initiative stem from the worldview labelled "gender and development", which emphasises that the societal inequities existing between men and women are structural. The present patriarchal social institutions enforce male dominance and marginalise women's interests. It is therefore, not enough to have only specific policy initiatives in the sectors which largely benefit women. "Merely incorporating women into the development process will not improve their welfare, but the process itself will have to be modified" (Folbre 1995). Radical changes are required to be made for gender empowerment in all institutions, laws, and property rights that perpetuate male domination. Incentive structures existing in social institutions influence "the empowerment of social groups designated by gender, nation, race, class, or other dimensions of collective identity" (Folbre 1994). Power is the ability to act and successfully participate in local and extra community decision-making (Reitzes *et al.*, 1980). The separate gender space created in the panchayats is thus expected to lead to a process of gender empowerment which includes: attempts to critically understand one's social environment, gain control in the community, obtain needed resources, establish gender coalitions and engage in other proactive behaviours.

An Anecdotal Aftermath

As is true with any legislation which is dissonant with the existing social hierarchies, the post-Amendment Act scenario has been filled with conflicts that are diverse and peculiar. "One, the conflict between local level politicians on one hand, and the State-level politicians and national-level politicians on the other: two, the conflict between bureaucracy and local level politicians; and three, the conflict between vested interests and local level politicians" (Mukherjee, 1994). What is apposite to the theme of this paper are the gender conflicts occurring in the third tier in the post Amendment era, between male vested interests and the first cohort of women panchayat functionaries. Patriarchal mind sets have hitherto denied women the opportunity of participating in panchayat affairs. This has cumulated their ignorance about the political and development processes operating at the grassroots. Patriarchy has reared its head with renewed vigour in the arena of panchayat politics after the Amendment Act. Despite being coerced by the Act, men are scarcely willing to relinquish their age-old control over these rural bastions of power. They are using both fair and foul means to subvert the process of shifting the locus of panchayat control into the hands of the new leaders. There are many instances where the erstwhile *Sarpanch*[2] has installed a woman member of his own family as the new village chief. In other cases, attempts have been made to intimidate women office bearers through sheer brute force.

For narrating some of the experiences of the first generation women panchayat functionaries, it is appropriate to begin with the story of Vasumati, the first woman sarpanch of village Lohara in Umerga block of Osmanabad district. She was an illiterate widow and belonged to the Scheduled Castes. Being landless, she eked out a living through labour on farm and construction sites. Subsequent to the Amendment, the seat of the village sarpanch was reserved for a woman from the Scheduled Caste community. Vasumati was popular choice of the village women because of her somewhat assertive nature. But the male panchayat members, especially the *upasarpanch*[3] would not concede to her tutelary powers. The *upasarpanch* waited for the day when Vasumati would resign and he would assume the reins of office.

Vasumati found all her efforts to negotiate with the menfolk set at naught. Her only ally was the peon who did the menial jobs for the village panchayat. He provided crucial support to her by being able to read and interpret official correspondence. It was not that Vasumati was without any *development vision.* She was able to prioritise the village needs and had her own ideas of how government funds had to be spent. But being illiterate and totally uninitiated into the working of the panchayat, she was constrained to repose some degree of faith in the peon. He became her trustworthy advisor. This sudden elevation in the status of the peon further fuelled the wrath of the other menfolk. The tensions in the village community thus grew bringing all development works to a halt. Vasumati's pleas to the *gram sevak* who lived 30 km away in Umerga fell on deaf ears.

The climax was reached when there was an exchange of blows between Vasumati and the *upasarpanch.* This physical assault prompted Vasumati to seek help from the District Collector, (who happened to be a woman) in Osmanabad, some 90 km away. In a village *gram sabha,* the village community, especially the panchayat members freely expressed their views to the District Collector. A clear picture of the political dynamics operating in the village community emerged. The menfolk stated that they were willing to tolerate a woman *sarpanch,* but not one who was under the guiding influence of the panchayat peon. It also emerged that the *gram sevak* seldom visited the village and had not convened any meeting of the new village panchayat. There was no government functionary or other individual available to facilitate the panchayat decision making processes and provide counsel to the *sarpanch* and other members. The absence of a facilitator constrained Vasumati, untrained in the art of panchayat politics, to depend upon her mentor- peon. Some elders lamented the fact that the village matters had come to such a head that outsiders had to intervene. After much debate, a consensual truce was reached and the *gram sevak* was persuaded (under duress!) to reside in the village.

Vasumati (may her tribe increase!) is one genre amongst the first generation functionaries in the post-Amendment period, who are naturally bold and remain undaunted in the face of the male animus confronting them. But their true political enfranchisement is inhibited by an amalgamation of factors, like: (a) illiteracy and political inexperience which constrains them to place their trust ultimately in one of the men themselves; (b) Machiavellian or obtrusive tactics on the part of the menfolk who contrive to bring about the fall of the likes of Vasumati, forcing them either to submit to male dictates or resign from office; (c) absence of a grassroots facilitator to provide support and make the process of political transition in village communities easier. Thus the Vasumatis of today, although eager to participate in the arena of panchayat politics, are in the end thwarted both by male "brain and brawn" and their own ignorance and political innocence.

Sudhama, the *sarpanch* of Hiwatga participated in a semi structured discussion along with Parvati of Patsangvi, Vimal of Ralesangvi and some women from these villages. All three women were illiterate and new entrants in the domain of panchayat politics. Their new roles, responsibilities and the expectations the village community had from their women chieftains were discussed. Sudhama belonged to the *Vanjari* tribe. Women from this community, according to Sudhama and the others are usually very outspoken. The gender equation in the *Vanjari* community is traditionally less skewed than in other non-tribal societies. Sudhama could not only verbalise better, but stated that being illiterate, she had learnt to listen better with her ears. She was aware of the different development programmes and could prioritise the development needs of her village. She stated that a drinking water well was the imperative need of her village. There were no bus services to her village since there was no road. Despite this, she went to the panchayat samity regularly, along with the *upasarpanch* to lobby for these development needs of her village. However, the corpus of funds available for her village was small. Asked about the difference her advent on the panchayat scene had made, the village women answered that there was now somebody who could understand their needs.

Like Vasumati, Sudhama is assertive and vocal about enforcing her right to participate in the village panchayat. Both can envision the development needs of their respective villages and enjoy the confidence of their community women. But Sudhama is more fortunate in belonging to a community where patriarchy is less rigid and women have historically played a less submissive role than in many other village societies. Both these women are existing in a state of awareness wherein they are able to assess and analyse the predicaments facing their villages. But they cannot engage in suitable proactive behaviours for different sets of reasons.

Sudhama, for the lack of resources and to some extent official indifference. And Vasumati for more complex reasons already discussed earlier. For this genre of women functionaries, it is important that capacity building interventions have to be directed at consolidating their natural self esteem. Efforts have to be made for broadening their *development vision* and creating a supporting environment for their endeavours.

Parvati, belonged to the *sutar* community, which is among the "Other Backward Castes." She was under the absolute control of her husband, the erstwhile *sarpanch*. Fearing that the post was going to be reserved for women, her husband had ensured that his wife got nominated for the office. Parvati was totally ignorant of her responsibilities, and was devoid of any urge to break her husband's stranglehold. The *Anganwadi* worker of Patsanghvi was also present. The latter stated that since September 1995 when Parvati had become *sarpanch*, the only perceptible change that had occurred on the development front was that the village women had been covered under DWCRA[4]. But the Worker and the other village women claimed that this was not due to Parvati's efforts. It emerged that the women reposed more faith in the worker than their new *sarpanch*.

Vimal's situation was similar to that of Parvati's. She belonged to the *kumbhar* caste and was illiterate, unable to read or write. She said with some pride that she had learnt to sign her name however, in the adult literacy classes organised in the village. And she affixed her signature on whatever paper the *upasarpanch* and her husband asked her to!

Like Parvati and Vimal, there are many more amongst the first cohort of women functionaries whose silences remain unheard. It is for training practitioners to hear them. This raises a host of concerns and challenges for the trainers. Should the learning approach be a conscientising (Frierian) one, which essentially leads to the learner's liberation from all forms of oppression, ignorance and dependency? In that case, it is necessary to anticipate the social conflicts that are likely to supervene. How are village communities and the women functionaries going to negotiate these conflicts?

Values in Training

During a discussion with a group of trainers from the Panchayat Raj Training Institutions in Maharashtra, one of them aptly remarked: "Our task is to make the women more competent and at the same time make the men understand the need for doing so." A veritable dilemma indeed! The trainers also narrated how the functionary's husband is inclined to insist that the panchayat affairs should be run according to his dictates. They also expressed concern about the indifference the functionary faced in her household not only from the male members but also from the womenfolk. The other womenfolk in the family were unwilling to extend support for child care and household chores so as to enable the functionary to attend panchayat meetings. Yet, despite these social impediments, the trainers said that the functionaries exhibited a tremendous urge to learn, especially about village panchayat governance.

Gender participation in the panchayats has obviously initiated a process of change which is in conflict with the prevalent social and political values. Many of the functionaries are oppressed (Freire 1970). This very context of training necessitates the use of a learning approach which cannot take a neutral stance in relation to the existing set of values. The whole process of learning through training will consist of increasing the ability of the functionaries to make decisions and exercise control over their environments. The methodology suggested by Paulo Freire consists of the dynamic praxis model leading to a continuous cyclic reflection and action dynamics. Anything that is learnt is put into action, followed by a process of scrutiny and evaluation through reflection and then further action.

The Freirian learning approach is a participative one and attaches great significance to learner participation. The "participation motivation" or the degree of readiness of these functionaries to participate in the learning process is crucial factor determining the success of the learning process. For the functionaries, the external social influence i.e the Amendment Act is affecting them equally. And the training exercise is a learning process consistent with the current needs of the women functionaries. However, these women are a mixed lot. Some like Sudhama and Vasumati are in a state of preparedness to avail of learning opportunities afforded through training. The explanation for their motivation is individual to them and the communities to which they belong. Women like Vimal and Parvati are less oriented towards learning. Thus there are concomitant forces of socialisation like household and community attitudes that an individual learner- functionary has to face and which determine her positive, negative or neutral valence towards learning through training (Rubenson 1975). Therefore, the levels of participation of the functionaries in training will differ considerably. The question is can trainers exercise some influence upon the forces determining learner-valence?

There are two principal sets of factors determining the learner valence of a functionary. The first set is obviously related to the nature of the learning approach and content of training. Considering the training context and the fact that most of the functionaries are existing today in an oppressed state, the Freirian learning approach seems to be the natural choice. The content of training has to be related to the practical realities existing at the grassroots. The trainers from Maharashtra especially mentioned about the interest the functionaries took in the sessions on social legislation. The second set of factors influencing the learner valence of a functionary are related to the attitudes of her spouse, household and community. It is true that popular acceptance of the functionary's public role will raise her learner valence. For trainers, this means that they have to address the task of creating advocacy for gender participation in the panchayats. The existing attitudinal obstacles can be mitigated through the use of the gender sensitising training modules for orienting the male panchayat functionaries, village-level workers, officers and others. This can be expected to set in motion a gradual process of attitudinal change in village communities.

Thus, the training process will indoctrinate the functionaries with the belief that the age-old male preserve of panchayat governance is not an inviolate one. It will also attempt to mitigate the existing social prejudices. It is important to understand that the path towards women's political enfranchisement is fraught with social conflicts. Therefore, trainers are commissioned with the delicate task of increasing women's ability to govern and at the same time enabling the menfolk to appreciate this new awakening.

Whither to Trainers?

The prevailing patriarchal dispositions of village communities and the political innocence of the first generation women functionaries are therefore, two critical considerations that shape the training paradigm. Trainers will thus have to work on a very extensive canvas in order to develop the political intellect of these women. Given the enormity of their task, it may be prudent to follow a system approach for planning the training process. This will make the training exercise better structured and customised to the needs of rural communities.

The first step is to recognise that the learning process initiated through training has to be both value and need based. The value content of training has already been discussed. The simple question to be asked is "what are the social and political values we want to promote through training?" These values flow from the mandate of Amendment Act and are related essentially to gender equity.

At the same time, it is necessary to design a need-based training exercise. The levels of knowledge and awareness of individual functionaries vary greatly. Any training activity has to be commensurate with individual needs. This will not only ensure learner- participation in training, but also make the whole exercise relevant to ground realities. The validity of the training paradigm will depend upon the degree to which all relevant need perspectives, including that of the adult learners are incorporated into it.

What are the other need perspectives? We have to consider besides the individual needs, those of the organisation and community. The Organisation in this context is the functionary's village panchayat. Her responsibilities as a panchayat member are clearly defined by legislation.

The organisational goals of the village panchayat are also clearly mandated by legislation. They embrace subjects related to both panchayat governance and village development. But the process of needs identification does not end here. The community specific needs also merit deliberation. Consider a tribal community with its own special problems of food insecurity and malnutrition. Functionaries of such communities need to understand the nature of interventions for alleviating such phenomena. Thus, the training process has to address the entire gamut of individual, organisational and community needs.

For reasons of practicality, trainers cannot treat this combined set of needs in an unrefined form, but have to synthesise it through some filters like: (a) the institutional purpose of the village panchayat i.e. whether the particular need is within the ambit of panchayat governance. The village panchayat has original jurisdiction over many developmental issues and only an advocacy role in many others. The functionary has to clearly envision her role in each of these two contexts; (b) *feasibility*, i.e. the fulfilment of particular goal would depend upon the nature and scope of the training process, the wherewithal of trainers and the knowledge level of the functionary. It would also depend on the degree of decentralisation i.e. whether the training is being conducted at the village level or in training colleges. This exercise will describe the core competencies which the new functionaries have to develop and, therefore, the content of training. More focus can be brought into the training exercise by following this screening process.

Conclusions

The post-Amendment scenario is expected to witness great advancements in the political and social emancipation of rural women. However, the first generation women functionaries have a long way to traverse before they eventually come of age in the sphere of panchayat politics. Today, they are mere novices in the art of grassroots governance. Their passage into ascendancy has to be nurtured by a careful process of capacity building. At the same time, it is necessary to ensure that the accompanying social conflicts do not charge the environment of traditionally patriarchal rural communities. Development trainers bear the twin burden of initiating the women panchayat functionaries into the complex art of panchayat governance; and of creating and sustaining a supporting social environment. Both these tasks are no doubt daunting, but imperative to realise the spirit of the Amendment Act. It remains to be seen to what extent trainers will be able to fulfil the onus of making gender participation meaningful in the panchayats.

NOTES

1. The panchayats are the rural institutions of local self-governance. The first tier is the Zilla Parishad at the district level, the second—the Panchayat Samity at the block level, and the third is the village panchayat.
2. The elected head of the village council or panchayat.
3. The deputy chief of the village panchayat.
4. A scheme called Development of Women and Children in Rural Areas under which women are encouraged to undertake group employment activities. They are provided with a working capital of Rs 25000 and also appropriate skill training.

REFERENCES

Freire, Paulo. (1970). *Pedagogy of the Oppressed.* New York: Seabury Press.

Folbre, Nancy. (1994). *Who Pays for the Kids? Gender and the Structures of Constraint.* New York: Routledge.

—— 1995. Engendering Economics: New Perspectives on Women, Work and Demographic Change. Annual World Bank Conference on Development Economics 1995. Editors: Bruno and Pleskovic. The World Bank, Washington D.C.

Mukerjee, Amitava (1994). Seventy-third Amendment: Next Steps and Conflict Resolution. *Decentralisation—Panchayats in the Nineties,* Edited by Amitava Mukherjee. Vikas Publishing House Pvt. Ltd. New Delhi.

Reitzes, Donald & Reitzes Dietrich, (1980). Saul D. Alinsky's Contribution to Community Development. *Journal of the Community Development Society,* vol. II no.2 Fall 1980, Illinois.

Rubenson, K. (1975). Participation in Recurrent Education. Centre for Educational Research and Innovations, Organisation for Economic Co-operation and Development, Paris.

6

WOMEN IN UTTARAKHAND
A Study of Work, Environment and Health of the Rural Women of the Himalayas

— ANJALI BAHUGUNA

The Himalayan range is the most populous mountain range in the world. Besides its cultural and ethnic diversity the people of the Himalayas face common difficulties. The central Himalayan region of Uttar Pradesh consists of eight districts, collectively known as Uttarakhand. The region covers 51,125 sq.km. area and is divided into two administrative divisions, Garhwal Mandal including five districts, Uttarkashi, Chamoli, Pauri, Tehri and Dehradun and Kumaon Mandal including the three districts, Almorah, Nainital and Pithoragarh. According to the 1991 census the total population of the eight districts of Uttarakhand was 59,26,146 with a density of population of 116 people per sq. km.

Women are an essential productive force in the economy of Uttarakhand. It is heartening that for the first time India's 1991 census has taken into account the contribution which women make to the national economy. The census records all their work viz. unpaid family labour, self employed, home based work, part time, casual work as productive work. However, the problem remains, whether the rural women were able to get their work recorded. Women in Uttarakhand are predominantly rural, poor and illiterate. They are less endowed in terms of health, education and productive assets.

Density of Population

Population, density is rapidly rising in the Hill Region. As per 1991 census, it has gone up to 116 against 95 in 1981 and 75 in 1971. Changes in the density varies from one district to the other.

In Uttar Pradesh and India, besides other usual factors responsible for the high rate of density the most important factor has been the cultivable land of the Gangetic plains. In rural areas agricultural production and cultivation still contributes high proportion of income generation. Illiteracy, social and cultural traditions did play an important role in raising the density of population in Uttar Pradesh and in India. The same proves true in Uttarakhand also. Since in rural areas usually women are left behind for agricultural and other work hence mostly more fertile areas have more density of population.

Most of the young people go out in search of employment to plains. In almost all rural areas the villages are mostly left behind with women, children and old men. If one travels to the remote rural area, it is evident that there are many villages where it is not possible to see young men. The economy is purely based on women's work and the yearly income which the young men bring when they come home during their vacation.

Problems and Constraints of Hill Agriculture

The problems and constraints of hill economy and rural women of the Uttarakhand have been discussed based on observations, interviews and focus group discussions.

Fragmented and Scattered Land Holdings

The average size of land holdings sometimes less than 1 hectare is very small. The average size of land holding (0.82 ha.) is even smaller about (0.50 ha) for cultivation of field crops, if the orchard holdings are excluded. Besides, these tiny holdings are fragmented and scattered over different hill terraces. As a result the farm development programmes cannot be effectively undertaken. These scattered holdings lead to strain and loss of time and energy of the rural women.

Degradation of Lands and Soil Erosion

Large scale deforestation has occurred in the area to meet the ever increasing demand for timber over the past several decades. Though this has been checked, still for fuel and fodder needs it is continuous to some extent. Animal are also left open for grazing causing further damage to vegetation and soil. During heavy rains the area faces soil erosion.

Fuel and Fodder Needs

The increasing population of both human being and animals is leading to ever increasing demand for fuel and fodder. The problem is more acute because of small holdings leaving hardly any scope for growing fodder crops and other such crops producing fuel and by-product. Thus, in the absence of alternative sources and large scale deforestation that has already occurred, meeting the demand for fuel and fodder needs in the hill areas has become an urgent and pressing problem.

Women on an average spend 6 to 7 hours each for collecting fuel for cooking in a village, in the evening all family members generally surround the fire. This fire acts as energy for working, heating, lighting in almost all households. Interviews of 200 household in the villages of district Tehri Garhwal revealed that the rural women were using logs, twigs, branches, shrubs, crop residues and cattle dung converted into dung cakes in their traditional *chullha* for cooking.

Based on general observation and at the same time asking the rural women how much distance they generally cover in fetching water, fuelwood and fodder women from 43 households stated that they usually cover 7 to 8 km. per day. The drudgery involved in this leaves them exhausted. Study of 200 households in the remote rural areas has shown that with low income, low education, low calorie food, the usually women headed families have to strive hard to meet their survival needs. Especially at higher altitudes rural women's main necessity becomes procurement of fuel for cold climate.

Inadequate Income and Employment Opportunities

The sixty-seven per cent of the total land area in Uttarakhand consists of the reserved forests and the agricultural land is merely 12.5 per cent. A majority of its inhabitants are marginal peasants. The employment opportunities in the hill is limited to crop cultivation and animal raising. Low agricultural productivity leads to low level of income. In general large number of people, almost all in the remote rural areas live much below the poverty line.

Major Agricultural Activities Performed by the Rural Women

Except ploughing the rest of the work is done by women only, such as the following

Levelling

Ensures a uniform distribution of seeds, manures and fertilizers. It is quite a difficult operation in the hill region, where the terraces are too steep.

Manuring

Manuring of the land after ploughing is one of the most labour intensive task. Rural women carry more than twenty head loads of manure. Each head load is approximately of 18 kg. In their agricultural land it is the women's work which is tiring.

Weeding

Regular weeding of the crops is carried out to ensure better crop growth and yield. Women perform this function with small hoes.

Harvesting

The crops are harvested by women. The sickle is the tool used for harvesting. This is quite a labour intensive work done by women.

Threshing

Farmers with large holdings thresh the harvested paddy or wheat crop through tampling by bullocks on threshing floor. In the case of marginal and small land holders paddy is threshed by foot smashing which leads to boils on the foot of women.

Winnowing

To separate the grains from the chaff, winnowing of the threshed grains is done by women only. Besides the above agricultural activities women also perform the food processing activities of sun drying of the produce, storage of the grains, dehusking the grains and turning the grains into flour.

Seasonal Farming Activities of the Rural Women
(An average estimate of activities in a year)

Month	Activities
January	Severe winter season, snow fall. No farming, only collection of fuel wood.
February	do
March	Preparing fields for paddy and jhingora.
April	Sowing paddy, jhingora, harvesting paddy.
May	Sowing Soyabean, Mandua, harvesting of wheat and massoor.
June	Harvesting of summer vegetables.
July	Weeding paddy, mandua and jhingora.
August	do
September	Harvesting paddy, maize, preparing field for wheat.
October	Sowing wheat, pea etc.
November	Harvesting of pulses, sowing wheat.
December	Harvesting of mustard.

Besides above agricultural activities women perform many other household chores, such as washing utensils, clothes, cleaning house, collecting fodder, milking buffalo, cutting grass, carrying stone, waking up hill with loads of fuel and grass and looking after the children and the old members of the family.

General Problems of the Rural Women

Living in the villages of the hill areas is not easy. Basic requirements of even a moderate living such as potable water, fuel wood, fodder, hospitals and maternity centres, veterinary services, schools, and vehicular transport, marketing and banking centres are not easily available. The far-flung habitations in the mountains remain largely secluded. The villages are of very small size and scattered far and wide. Electricity is unknown in a large part of the remote rural areas of Uttarakhand. Sometimes even kerosene oil is also not available in the remote far off villages. Rural women's main reponsibilities are fetching water, fuel, fodder, routine unavoidable chores of household, besides looking after and nursing old ones and children. Over-occupied with breeding and nursing in the far off villages, the rural mothers have no time even to think about their own comforts, status recognition and independent career.

Though during the planning era much has been done for the development of women yet it will take time for these rural women of the villages to get the benefits of the development strategy of the government

Male Migration and it Consequences

The phenomenon that is unique to the hills of U.P. is the heavy male out-migration. Male migration has become a basic survival necessity and an accepted way of life in the hills since money earned by out-migrants contributes significantly to the economic resources of the family. In two remote rural villages of district Tehri Garhwal a survey was undertaken and the researchers stayed with the rural families. The conclusion was derived that 70 per cent of the total hill households, the male head of the households is a long time migrant, and 30 per cent of the households men are seasonal migrants. During the prolonged absence of the husband the women take all the responsibilities, economic, health, social and other kinds for their families.

Migration is a common feature in many Third World Countries. This global exodus of men leaves a growing number of women managing alone in the countryside. In some parts of rural Africa the figures are dramatic, with over 40 per cent of households in Kenya, Botswana, Ghana and Sierra Leone headed by women. In Latin America, too, substantial number of households in both urban and rural areas are run by women: a third in Jamaica, for instance and a fifth in Peru, Honduras, Venezuela and Cuba.

These women are doubly disadvantaged. They are often left without help at crucial times of the year, having to manage the ploughing, the planting, and harvesting on their own with as much help as their relatives and children can spare.

Since hill agriculture relies on human muscle power, many of the operations in rural production and services are performed by children chiefly by female children who leave school. The migration is limited to males only in the villages. Females work on farm and look after the families. With the migration of males, the productive manpower base of the villages is eroded and the vicious circle of low production and poverty continues. Most of the men folks serve in army, police and other Government and private enterprises. Generally educated as well as uneducated youths move out in search of employment in the large cities of the country like Delhi, Bombay, Lucknow, Kanpur etc. It is one of the causes for more female per 1000 males in the rural areas of district Chamoli, Tehri, Pauri, Almora and Pithoragarh.

Health of the Rural Women

Illness in the rural areas is caused by the lack of clean drinking water and sanitation. Malnutrition affects, the health of the children and women of members of the family and makes them more vulnerable to disease. Often, an elder child, who may be a few years older than the infant, is left to take care of the young ones. Without proper supervision by the mothers the children are not fed properly and may develop symptoms, leading to one or more deficiency diseases.

There is close relationship between health, economy and social progress. Foods contain a number of nutrients. When sufficient quantities of the right type of foods are not eaten, many essential nutrients are not available in adequate quantities to the body. This leads to the development of several diseases. Some of the common deficiency diseases found are protein-energy malnutrition (PEM), Vitamin A deficiency, anemia due to lack or poor absorption of iron and Vitamin B complex deficiency. In rural communities, especially the children are nursed by mothers over long periods and supplementary foods essential to prevent PEM are not provided at the proper age. Besides protein energy malnutrition (PEM) another principal nutritional problem is Vitamin A deficiency. A direct result of vitamin A deficiency is impairment of vision ultimately leading to blindness. Lack of vitamin A results in stunted growth and abnormalities of bones and teeth. Deficiency of iron causes anemia. Anemia is widespread in women of child bearing age and children. Some of the common manifestations of Vitamin B complex deficiency are sore mouth, sore tongue. It also leads to gastro intestinal infections such as diarrhoea and dysentery. Goitre, a disease related to iodine deficiency, is prevalent in the Himalayan region. Goitre results in enlargement of the thyroid gland. Apart from retardation in physical growth, lack of mental development is also observed in these cases.

Women in labour are usually tended by women. In rural areas they rely on traditional methods only, passed down through the generations from mother to daughter. Although majority of women deliver safely but many die during childbirth. Many of them who survive have to live on with the scars of difficult pregnancy, displaced or weak wombs, cycles of debilitating infections, exhaustion and bleeding. Many women's bodies are in a very weak state when they feel the first pains of labour.

It is rare to see a hospital along with doctor and proper staff and medicines in the remote rural areas. Only the traditional beliefs and skill and faith in their local gods and goddess is the remedy of their diseases and sickness.

In the rural areas of district Tehri Garhwal, while working in a project 'Technology Programme and Women, A Study of Women in Garhwal Himalaya' it was found on the basis of discussion that long hours of walking and carrying heavy loads leads to great physical strain. Postural defects like bent backs, pain in legs, calf muscles, pain in arms and shoulders becomes a common feature. Carrying water from long distances leads to intense pain in hip bones, waist, shoulders and different parts of the body. Cooking in small kitchens full of smoke leads to irritation of eyes, nose and throat, cough, bronchitis, eye diseases, exhaustion physical pain, headaches etc. Besides the common features available with regard to health were water problems and water borne diseases, iodine deficiency disorders and respiratory track infections. Preservation and strengthening of indigeneous systems of medicine as the wealth of knowledge on traditional medicine still exists in the region. The rural women cure themselves and take care of their children in this traditional way.

Women and Environment

Probably no other group is more affected by environmental destruction than poor village women. For them every dawn brings with it a long march in search of fuel, fodder and water. Forests provide them food, fodder, fuel, and livelihood. Soil, water and air are three important bases of life. The lives of the rural women revolve very closely around the availablility of natural resources and the destruction of these natural resources bring about extremely harsh and immediate problems. The protests of the Chipko women show this clearly.

The Chipko movement in the Garhwal-Himalaya brought out the critical role of women in sustaining eco-development. As a matter of fact this movement has been described as a feminist movement. 'Chipko' means 'hugging'. It started in 1973, to protect the forests from exploitative commercial policies in the form of protest against felling of trees. While in Reni (Chamoli district) the protest was against a timber contractor in all other cases the protest was against cash hungry men, who could not think and care the loss of the forests. They could not realise how their women had to walk for many more miles to collect this daily load of fuel and fodder. In district Tehri women put mud plaster on deep and illegal cuts in pine trees for the extraction of resin *(Lisa)*. Chipko movement originated from the local issues. 'Chipko' is now a household word and has an irresistable idea for the protection and conservation of forests which are vitally, linked with the life of forest dwellers.

Village women are quite intelligent also. They know very well that in a particular geographic situation, only specific trees or vegetation should be grown, so that appropriate needs of fertiliser, soil, water and energy can be met. It is axiomatic that only people living near forests can establish a practical and harmonious relationship with the forests. The minimum needs of the rural women living next to the forests, who have been customarily using them for their survival and their village economy have to be given importance and the administration should be such that these rights are exercised easily by them. The Centre for Science and Environment has produced two comprehensive citizens' Reports on the "State of India's Environment". The clear conclusion of these movements and voluntary effort is that to arrest environmental degradation and promote sustainable use of environment, people's participation at the grassroot level, particularly of the rural women must be ensured in the control and management of natural resources.

The negative impact of the big dams, the hill women think, is largely on them as their lives are dependent largely on their immediate environment. As a result of displacement the rural women face total social, cultural and psychological collapse. Amongst the strongest opponents of the Tehri Dam are the thousands of people mostly the rural women of the villages in the submersion area who depend on their homeland and do not know much where and how they will be rehabilitated.

A critical issue and a point of conflict between local people and state agencies is around energy. The main source of energy in the mountains is hydro-energy which is increasingly. being captured, for purposes of generation of hydroelectric power. Although the Himalayan region has vast potential, this potential is limited by the fact that the area lies on seismically active zone and unsuitable for large dam construction. Small run-off-the river schemes are more environmentally appropriate and can generate energy for both local use and for export. A second energy source is in the form of fuelwood and biomass. This is the primary source of energy for the local population. Women endure great stress in the collection of fuelwood for cooking and it is compounded by the need for collection of fodder and water. Development of alternative biomass based energy sources and the extension of non-conventional energy sources are the priorities in the planning.

In the end to conclude it is appropriate to say that women must fully participate in the policies being made now and through the decade.

REFERENCES

Agarwal, A., Chopra, R., Sharma, K. (1982). The State of India's Environment, *The First Citizen's Report*, New Delhi.

Agarwal, A., *et al.*, (1985). The State of India's Environment, (1984-85). *The Second Citizen's Report*, New Delhi.

Anker, R. (1983). "Female labour force participation in developing countries: a critique of current definitions and data collection methods," *in International Labour Review*, November-December.

Bahuguna, Anjali (1995). *Science and Technology in Relation to Rural Women* (Ed.) Har Anand Publications, New Delhi.

Bahuguna Sunderlal, Chipko Message (1994). *Whither Development?* Chipko Information Centre, Parvatiya Navjivan Mandal Siliyara (Tehri Garhwal), India.

Bandyopadhyay, J. and D. Gyawali (1994). Himalayan Water Resources : Ecological and Political Aspects of Management. *Mountain Research and Development*, Vol.14, Nov. 1.

Bhatt, C.P. (1980). *Ecosystem of the Central Himalaya and Chipko Movement*, Gram Swarajya Sangh, Gopeshwar, Chamoli, U.P.

Boserup, E. (1970). *Women's Role in Economic Development*, New York, St. Martin's Press.

Census of India : 1981.

Census of India : 1991.

Govt. of India, *Planning Commission*, First Five Year Plan (1951-1956).

Govt. of India, *Planning Commission*, Second Five Year Plan (1956-1961).

Govt. of India, *Planning Commission*, Fourth Five Year Plan (1969-1974).

Govt. of India, *Planning Commission*, Fifth Five Year Plan (1974-1979).

Govt. of India, *Planning Commission*, Sixth Five Year Plan (1980-1985).

Govt. of India, *Planning Commission*, Seventh Five Year Plan (1985-1990).

Govt. of India, Planning Commission, Eighth Five Year Plan (1992-1997).

Joshi, P.C. (1995). *Uttarakhand Issues and Challenges*, Har Anand Publication, New Delhi.

Shramshakti (1983). Report of the National Commission on Self Employed Women and Women in the Informal Sector, Delhi.

Singh O.P. (Ed.) (1983). *Himalaya : Nature Man and Culture*, Rajesh Publication, New Delhi.

Valdiya, K.S. (ed.) (1988). *Kumaon : Land and People*, Gyanodaya Publication, Nainital.

COMMUNITY INTERACTIVE PROCESSES APPROACHES AND INSIGHTS

7

COMMUNITY PARTICIPATION IN KUSIYARA WATERSHED PROJECT

— HARI GOVIND SINGH

This paper is based on the experience of Kusiyara Watershed Project (KWP), which was implemented in Kusiyara village of Mirzapur district in Uttar Pradesh. The main objective of the project was to generate and sustain community participation to identify local developmental problems, the ways to resolve them by various means. Some of the main needs identified were:

— Improvement of environment and ecological balance and restoration of natural resources.
— Work for land development and assure more food production.
— Ensure availability of potable water.
— Devise new sources for income generation.
— To set land records straight and ensure land title to insecure land holders amongst poorest of the poor.
— To minimize migration of villagers to neighbouring disricts/ states by giving them gainful employment within the area.

Implementation Strategy

As soon as District Rural Development Agency (DRDA). Mirzapur released the first instalment of Rupees Five Lakhs to Arthik Anusandhan Kendra (AAK) on 25.5.95, it immediately swung into action to conduct meeting at Kusiyara village. In the meeting a formal announcement regarding approval of watershed project and the receipt of first instalment amount was made. Both AAK and the villagers unanimously decided to take up work on field bunding subject to completion of measurement/demarcation and land records of families. They jointly decided in principle that 50 per cent of the wages earned from work would be contributed towards Kusiyara Watershed Development Fund (KWDF) and this fund would subsequently be utilized for future development programmes of the community and in the maintenance of watershed project.

Consequent upon this decision, management power of the fund was vested in Kusiyara Watershed Committee (KWC) and the assessment of work was done on weekly basis by the Secretary of AAK in consultation and guidance of KWC. Based on assessment of progress amount for wages was withdrawn from bank and disbursed to beneficiaries by the President, KWC in presence of members and the villagers. The Treasurer of KWC ensured timely collection of assured contribution from the wages of beneficiaries and collection of deposits in the Bank in the presence of Secretary, AAK. The record of contribution in respect of beneficiaries was retained by KWC and AAK office. Besides, each beneficiary was in receipt of a pink coloured contribution card which reflected date-wise detail of contribution alongwith signatures of the Secretary thereon.

Kusiyara Watershed Committee was given sole responsibility to prioritise list of beneficiaries for bunding and proper utilization of WDF. Guided by watershed staff, committee prioritised areas and issues. KWC was not guided by physical targets alone, but by the objective of achieving sound, cost-effective results. Farmers were engaged to work on their own lands to reduce cost and improve performance. Technical expertise was given to ensure construction of sound structures. However, farmers also gave approval of the design of structures in their own fields. Participation was recognized as crucial to the success of watershed efforts. This encouraged rural people to undertake activities which earlier were done entirely by outsiders before arrival of AAK. Farmers were empowered right from the start to use their appraisal and knowledge. These participatory approaches became significant in the generation of sustainable livelihood.

On last day of each month. Watershed Development Association (WDA) in its meeting reviewed work performance and discussed problems arising in work. Solutions were found amicably after thorough discussions. Time to time evaluation was done to further improve quality of work.

Mistakes

In the early implementing phase, due to unaccountability of target group and lack of encouragement, there was a sharp decline in the credibility of work progress as a result of which their dependency on AAK increased. AAK was determined not to repeat this in future.

There was no economic programme directly associated with development needs of the women community. It adversely affected their participation skills at various levels of work. AAK intensified motivation to integrate women with economic and income generating programmes relating to procurement and direct marketing of minor forest produce which was identified to be a strong and useful resource for income. Women were being constantly motivated to undertake field exposure to gain knowledge and experience. WDF constituted by KWC was utilised to accomplish this work. In the absence of proper knowledge and relevant experience expected community participation in the early implementation phase could not be extracted from community. This taught AAK how to train and work for capacity building of the team of committed workers.

Stage of Capacity Building

With embracing of errors, workers active involvement in watershed work has generated widespread awareness among target groups about their land rights and they are visibly motivated to strengthen their own village organizations. Raising awareness, information dissemination and community organization through training and developing skills, exposure and networking is being reinforced and activated. The following factors are attributed to enhanced capabilities of social activists of AAK.

(i) Regular training, exposure to problems emerging from community participation during programme implementation and discussions to evolve solution has helped build capacity for programme implementation.
(ii) Exposure visit to Ralegaon Sidhi, Paani Panchayat in Maharashtra from 27 November to December 1995 with success story and their work impact on community has enriched workers both in knowledge and experience.
(iii) Timely implementation of AAK's role in land transfer activities and district administration's valued cooperation has generated

new confidence and sense of optimism in villagers.

(iv) A trip to "SHARMS" in Daltongunj (Bihar) by community representatives and AAK activists from 24 September to 28 September 1995 and their exposure to lasting impact of work has further made them knowledgeable about various aspects of application and management of watershed programme. Committee members are motivated to transfer their knowledge to their respective communities.

(v) Selection of beneficiaries, be it bunding or community works like water resources and implementation of plan was carried out by KWC who prioritises entire work and decide on use of constituted WDF. So far, fourteen beneficiaries were given loan of Rs. 9150.00. KWC owns responsibility to ensure its repayments.

(vi) All physical targets—bunding, streams, repairs/deepening of old wells and selection of working team was done by KWC.

Achievements

In spite of several problems, AAK has achieved results with the cooperation of district administration, KWC and the villagers and work, as listed below, have been successfully accomplished.

(i) So far, appx. 400 poor tribals families were covered by *patta* and land demarcation. For remaining about 200 families, land records and demarcation work is in full swing and is expected to be over after monsoons are over. After this has been achieved, *pattas* will be distributed to the above mentioned families.

(ii) Minimum Wage Act was strictly being followed by AAK in all its development work. This attracted villagers all around a great deal who were now voicing their protest to local contractors against low payments of wages. This evoked wide response and sense of awareness in poor tribals in terms of their demand for minimum wage and better working conditions.

(iii) Main staple food of the people of Kusiyara village is 'Kodo', wheat is consumed rarely and rice only during functions and festivals. With more villagers resorting to field bunding, preventing soil erosion, tribals are now shifting to paddy cropping.

(iv) Labour migration to neighbouring districts/State were reduced to considerable extent as villagers were able to find work within the village in watershed work programme.

(v) This change helped in bringing down cases of bondage in the area as villagers and tribal community in particular, were engaged in watershed work and were not drawn to moneylenders for occasional financial needs.

(vi) So far 1,67,312 cubic feet earth work was completed.

(vii) Out of the total wages of Rs 51,503.10 paid to beneficiaries so far, KWC was able to raise Watershed Development Fund to the tune of Rs 22,354.00 which accounts for 43.4 per cent of the total wages paid towards people's contribution.

(viii) Total mandays so far were 1560.70 and rural tribal women's participation in entire programme was 771 which is 49.4 per cent.

(ix) Bunding was completed to cover 42 bighas of land to benefit 12 Kol tribals and Baiga tribe families during the period under reporting.

Problems in Implementation

(i) Presence of local contractors, exploiting class and villagers own prejudices did hamper work occasionally.

(ii) As women can play a pivotal role in society motivation, development process, involving women in development activities, was slow. There were problems in seeking women participation in community representation and decision making. This is perhaps due to their experience of age long exploitation and sex discrimination which eventually made them withdrawn and passive.

(iii) Especially during the monsoon road to the area of work becomes unsafe and inaccessible, difficulty is experienced in ensuring timely payment of wages to beneficiaries at field office.

(iv) Evidently, villagers had not been exposed to watershed project of any kind in the past in which their participation could be sought. This is their first hand experience and, therefore, they do not always seem to appreciate and visualise the concept of people's participation in the community based development programmes like this one.

(v) In the absence of proper knowledge and experience among members of KWC, they have their apprehensions about the sincerity and commitments of AAK in matters of finance and accounts. Therefore, AAK fears villagers' dependency on organization in the management of Watershed Development Fund.

Impact of Programme

On Village

Suppressed and exploited from ages, tribals of Kushiyara are now able to address their problems to various development agencies and work in participation with AAK. This has resulted in increase in the confidence and credibility of AAK. Villagers are able to appreciate work and authenticity of the organization and are motivated enough to join hands with AAK in community development work. Employment in watershed work is ensured and their migration from village is minimised. Privileged class finds it unable to influence decisions in matters concerning land/*patta* issues. Tribals are more united today and they seem undaunted and undeterred in even most trying situation created by the privileged class.

This programme has improved productivity of cultivated land, bringing fallow land under the plow, increasing the area under irrigation through efficient use of run off water and hence improving the sustainability of the system. A total of 95 families have so far been covered to benefit from bunding of their fields measuring 106.12 hectares stretched to six micro watersheds.

On Other Villages

The impact of Kushiyara work on neighbouring villages is overwhelming. There is growing pressure from nearby villages who are encouraged with results of ongoing watershed programme (of Kushiyara) to launch similar project in their areas. Villagers from new areas are assuring us of fullest community participation on lines of Kushiyara.

On Government Works

Government contractors feel pressurised by the ongoing watershed programme to implement minimum wage act in their respective areas of operation. Government departments are responding more positively to the needs of village pressure groups for allotment of land *pattas*.

On Other Programmes/Workers

In other fields like education, organization and awareness, villagers are inclined towards NRM and their interest is growing ever since. This serves as a moral booster among AAK workers and they are more determined and dedicated in carrying out their work.

8

COMMUNITY INTERACTIONS IN DISCOVERY OF A RURAL SLUM

— AMITAVA MUKHERJEE

Introduction

It was the month of June 1996. A group of my colleagues and myself were touring, in the hot blistering sun, Eastern Uttar Pradesh. To be precise, we were in the Districts of Ghazipur and Sultanpur, in search of a "least developed" area to start an integrated rural, repeat rural, development project. The intention was to tackle the structural causes of poverty. The structural causes generally accepted are lack of access to, or control over productive resources; powerlessness against both man and nature; alienated and marginalised by social factors; live in environmentally damaged lands; oppressed by State machinery and failure of public policy and the like.[1] This search led us from the remote villages like Balgarha in Kurebhar Block of Sultanpur, to the now famous "Ram Janmabhoomi Temple" at the site of the "Babri Masjid—that was"—in Ayodhya.

On June 25th we landed up at village Saddopur in Barachawar Block, Ghazipur District. Just on the day we were approaching the village, torrential rain had lashed the area. The first burst of a monsoon, after an extremely hot summer. The sweet smell of the parched earth drenched by raindrops, must have been a relief for many. But the discomfort of being drenched to our bones, gave us no cause for cheer.

The Village

To have an understanding of the village we moved at random in the village. A group of villagers accompanied us in the walk. They were very informative. They were extremely courteous. The walk through the muddy village lanes, taught us how to walk on slippery earth. "Dug our toes in the mud to avoid a fall", was the first lesson we learnt. We learnt about the trees. The great Jamun was plenty. The Seesam, Mangoes, Jackfruit and an occasional bamboo bush were all there. Our wandering through the meandering narrow village lanes was a lesson to remember. The village was stratified according to class. Big land owners and the politically powerful people, had their dwellings along the better pathways; they had drinking water sources nearer to their homes; they had easier access to the village; they owned most of the land.

The Chamar Tolla

The village was also stratified along caste lines. The lower castes were isolated in parts of the village. Chamars were one such caste. They belong to what is called the scheduled castes. With our mission to work for the marginalised groups, we thought the problem of the Chamars perfectly fit our scheme of things. Believing that those who belonged to scheduled castes are the ones economically backward, we proceeded to explore the rural problems of the "Chamar Tolla"—a collection of houses of Chamars in the village and seek their solutions. By the time we arrived at the Chamar Tolla, the torrential rains had turned into a fading drizzle. But our Chamar Tola had the look of a coastal village hit by a tidal wave : flooded to the "brim" with the crumbling huts and some large trees jutting out of the muddy water like punctuation marks on the scribbling pad of a school kid. When we arrived at the village, the villagers had gathered and knew of our arrival.

The Start

A social map of the village, we thought, would give us a convenient point of departure to start our "work". We made a round of the village through its narrow lanes. But we made little progress. With knee deep water all round, it was a sight to see its everything except the huts and a few water buffaloes under water. There was no way we could locate vegetation; drains were indistinguishable from bridle paths; cowsheds and "kitchens" looked alike. Nevertheless we did struggle through the muddy water and ankle-deep slush and mud, at least to have a fleeting glimpse of how our Chamar Tolla is organised.

The Tolla is no more than random congregation of huts and hutments. All thatched and mostly of old mud walls, some needing severe repairs. The heavy downpour had imprinted fresh marks of water channels on the mud walls; some deep, some less so. A bridle path ran all around the Chamar Tolla, enveloping a not so large cluster of huts. Whereas on the East-West segment of the bridle path, huts were located on one side only, to your right if your were moving from East to West. Along the North-South segment of the bridle path, huts lined both sides of the bridle path. No resemblance of habitation following any pattern was visible. The watery mess prevented us from figuring out what factors have dictated the configuration of the Tolla as it stood today.

When we completed our round, we reached a flat piece of land dominated by a large Neem tree, in front of the Balwadi Kendra, run by an NGO, Purvanchal Gramin Vikas Evam Prashikshan Sansthan (PVGPS). This was the place from where we began our walk as well. There was on this piece of land, the sole tubewell in the village. This Balwadi was one of the very few brick houses in our Tolla. We drew the sketch map of the village. It is in Figure 8.1.

There was no waterlogging here and a fairly large number of villagers, including women and children had assembled. Though the place was muddy, the villagers and we thought it was the driest place to learn and share something with the villagers. We entered into a dialogue with the assembled folks.

The ice breaker was to start washing our hands and feet plastered by mud, cowdung and what have you, at the tubewell, we mentioned earlier, Men, women and children and we "outsiders", all together went into a cleansing binge. It was such an excitement. The sheer joy of doing something together. Like a continuing thread all of us together, started "exploring" ways and means to settle down and carry-out a dialogue: some simple *baath-cheeth*. The small piece and parcel of land in front of the Balwadi was indeed the only choice but where to squat. The villagers soon produced all wooden cots (called *chaukies* in local dialect), and *khatias,* cots with ropes densely woven across a rectangular wooden frame, of every description and size. enough to stock a small village museum).

As we were settling down, the voice decibel of conversations started rising and soon reached a crescendo. It was difficult to have a meaningful interaction in such an excited atmosphere. The problem was soon converted into an opportunity; "since verbal interaction was

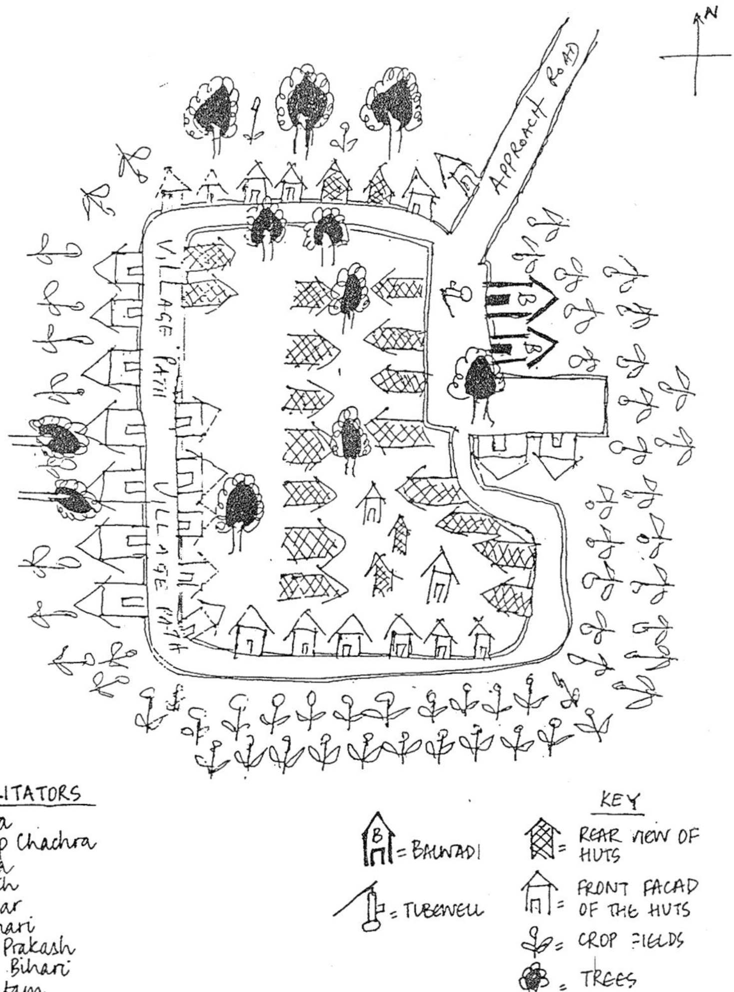

FIG. 8.1: Sketch Map of Chamar Tolla Village: Saddopur, district, Ghazipur

difficult, could we get down to some writings and figures", was the suggestion. The Balwadi came in handy in providing some chalk.

The two issues that had to be settled before the chalk could be put to good use: where to write and who should hold the chalk? There were no portable blackboards. The ground was too muddy to hold any mark or writings. An old man, half clad but apparently drunk, looked at our baffled faces. He had an easy solution. "Write on some of the *chaukis"*. And he identified a youth smarting a colourful shirt, who had left school—a "school drop out" in our terminology—who could be our *kaith* (one who could write for you). The stage was set for what turned out to be an exciting learning.

The Landscape

From the clamouring and animated discussions, strands of a volley of problems that confronted the Tolla on that wet and soggy afternoon emerged. We suggested to our "old man", if he could call the "house to order" and got the people to discuss whatever they wanted to. The discussants responded with ease. They were trying to articulate whatever their common problems were.

The young man with the chalk got activated and in consultation with several others started jotting down on a *chauki* what was being stated. The list, as in Figure 8.2 soon emerged on the *chauki.* We tried to understand how these could be possible These looked unfamiliar to rural development workers.

Where is the dominance of problem of low income? Low productivity? Basic health? What about food security? No, not good enough. Then land rights? Still not high on the agenda. Basic education? Yes, somewhere in the agenda. Minimum wages? A non-issue. Quite a challenging paradox we thought in an interior village in Eastern Uttar Pradesh.

All this while the women were sitting apart, and in a feudal situation, the women sitting with men (some of them being outsiders) to deliberate on community's problem was blasphemous. Our entreating did not help matters. Eventually a Balwadi teacher who was busy playing with the children amongst those assembled, came to our rescue. Once she volunteered to chip in, the women found it easy to crowd around the *chauki.* Explanations flowed from the crowd of how each of the problems impinge on the largely static life of that small hamlet. They were jotted down against each problem to give it a face; a unique meaning.

PROBLEMS	EXPLANATIONS
1. INTERNAL CONFLICTS	THOUGH ALL THE INHABITANTS WERE CHAMARS, QUARREL AND FIGHTS WERE COMMON.
2. LACK OF UNITY AMONG VILLAGERS	THE VILLAGERS PLACED INDIVIDUAL INTEREST ABOVE COMMUNITY INTEREST.
3. LACK OF PROPER APPROACH ROAD	THE EXISTING APPROACH WAS A MUD PATH WHICH IS A FAIR WEATHER ROAD.
4. LACK OF PROPER VILLAGE PATHS	THE VILLAGE PATHS DISAPPEARED DURING RAINS. THEY WERE KUICHA ROADS.
5. PROBLEM OF DRINKING WATER	THERE WAS ONLY ONE TUBEWELL. THE PEOPLE FETCH WATER FROM FAR AWAY VILLAGES.
6. NO PRIMARY SCHOOL	
7. LACK OF YEAR ROUND EMPLOYMENT LEADING TO SEASONAL MIGRATION.	THE YOUTH AND "THE LIKES" OF THE PERSON WHO WROTE THIS TABLE HAD NO EMPLOYMENT OPPORTUNITIES.
8. LANDLESSNESS	THE CHAMARS OWNED ONLY HOMESTEAD LAND. VERY FEW HAD LAND FOR CULTIVATION.
9. LACK OF ELECTRICITY	THERE WAS NO ELECTRICITY IN THE TOLLA.
10. PROBLEM OF DWELLING	THE HUTS WERE IN A STATE OF DISREPAIR. THEY COULDNOT GAIN ACCESS TO INDIRA AWAS YOJANA.
11. SANITATION	THERE WAS NONE OF IT EXCEPT NATURE
12. DRAINAGE	THERE WAS NO DRAINAGE SYSTEM. THE UPPER CASTE PEOPLE WHOSE LAND CIRCUMSCRIBED THE TOLLA WOULD NOT ALLOW WATER TO DRAIN OFF INTO THEIR LAND.

FIG. 8.2: Problem Tree of Chamar Tolla Village: Saddopur; district, Ghazipur

Was it at all possible to sort out the problems in some order of priorities? Could we pick up the most hated and biggest problem from the list? Could we then locate the one that does not top the list, but comes next to it? And then the next and so on? Thus proceeded our interviewing the "charter of problems". There were considerable confrontations. The discussion was animated but ranking was not easy verbally. The villagers then combined their chalk writing with Neem leaves. They devised their system of ranking. There were twelve problems charted out. The problem which has to be the first amongst the twelve, would have the highest number of leaves pitted against it, was the decision. The villagers elected to place twelve leaves against "internal conflicts" and just one short, against "lack of unity among the villagers".

The process went on till leaves appeared against the problem. The placing of the number of leaves against the problems depended on their gravity, a reconsideration ensued. Leaves started moving up and down the "ladder". Interestingly each of the problems had, at the first instance, a unique number of leaves to reckon with. Subsequent discussion and debate led to quite a bit of shuffling around. In the final analysis problem got clubbed. For instance, drainage and sanitation had the same "nuisance value" to the inhabitants of our Chamar Tolla. And then "non-availability of electricity" was bracketed with the problems associated with "landlessness" as giving the same intensity of "headaches (or heartaches)" to the villagers. The final scenario is the one shown in Figure 8.3.

Findings

The problems and their ranking has been an eye opener. A slum is not an urban phenomenon. A slum can be a rural phenomena as well. Here we are in our Chamar Tolla in Saddopur village in a rural slum. What then are the typical problems of a slum? Is rural poverty different from urban poverty? Is it necessary to distinguish the two forms of poverty? It would be useful to deal with these issues first, to which we may now turn.

First amongst the problems faced by the urban slums relate to the environmental domain. The special environmental problems faced by the urban poor result from, *inter alia,* competition for land, high living densities and overcrowded housing in hazardous areas; the speed of urban growth and the inadequate speed of clean water supply, sanitation and waste disposal services. Urban settlements come up in order to

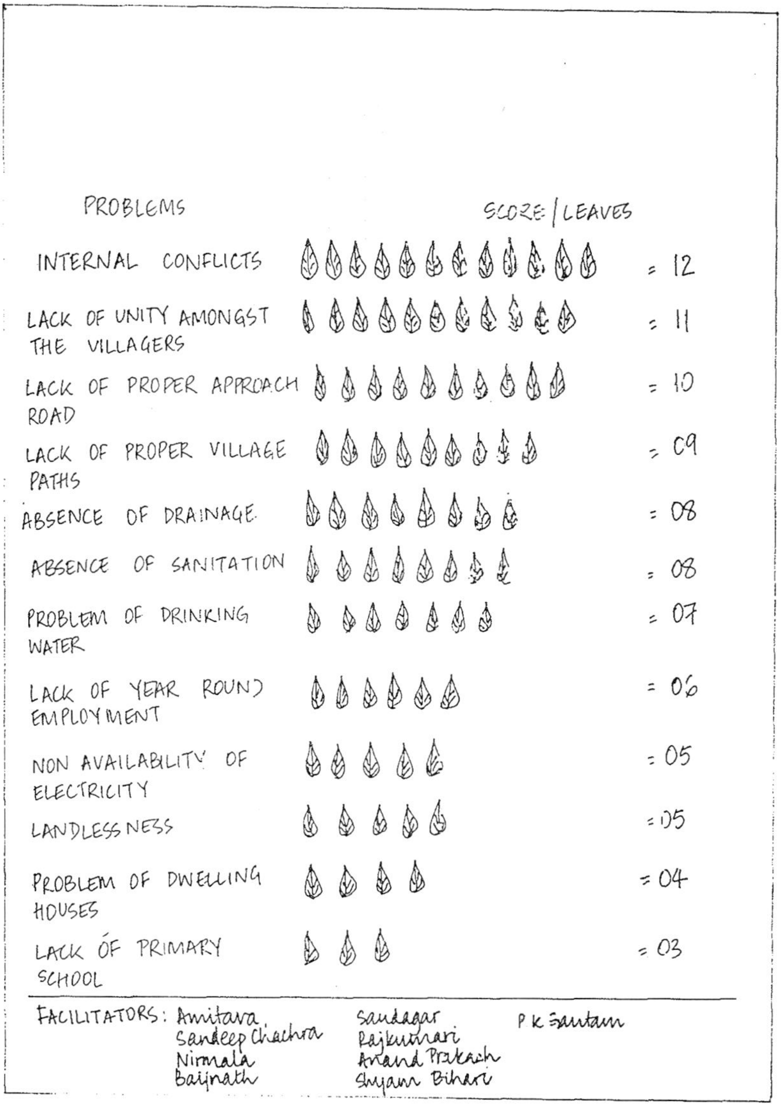

FIG. 8.3: Problem Prioritisation of Chamar Tolla Village: Saddopur, district, Ghazipur

group capitalist enterprises in a cost effective spatial configuration.[2] And people come to the cities in search of work. Health risks in urban slums include typhoid, cholera, diarrhoeal diseases, intestinal worms, diseases associated with poor drainage and waste disposal; :berculosis, influenza and meningitis associated with poor ventilation and overcrowding; respiratory diseases associated with open fires and poor ventilation; flooding and poor mobility for disabled people in neighbourhoods with poor accessibility.[3]

The second set of problems faced by the urban slums arise out of vulnerability from commercial exchange. Generally urban areas are characterised by a greater degree of commercialisation than rural areas. People are more reliant on market exchange to acquire basic goods and services and to earn money to have command over these goods and services, viz., water, food, rent which are generally either free or cheaper in rural areas. Commercialisation is more ubiquitous in the urban context than in the rural landscape. And it impinges upon all three aspects of the "trinity of deprivation" as crucial aspects of urban poverty: local economy, housing and education.[4] Like their rural counterpart,labour is probably the only saleable asset that the rural poor have. That is why, they are extremely vulnerable to changes in the demand for labour and the price of basic goods. This is often accentuated by the fact that most of the poor are employed by the informal sector. The earnings in the informal sector are typically irregular and often low. Casualisation and subcontracting make employment in the informal sector insecure.[5] What the urban labourer finds irksome is the disagreeableness of the work, or the unfair rewards.

Unemployment itself is a major cause of vulnerability. A few days out of job means a serious blow. It is also held that instability associated with the commoditization process reinforces poverty, and commercialisation tends to increase poverty amongst the poorest members of the urban community.[6]

The third category of urban problems relate to social stratification, fragmentation and crime. Urban slums have population from different ethnic, cultural and linguistic origins. There is a diversity of household types. The growing phenomenon of urban "street children", associated with poverty and family breakdown is characteristic of urban slums.[7] Social diversity often creates new tensions and survival strategies. Human relationship are more impersonal in urban areas; lifestyles, kinship and neighbcurhood or community support are different from those in rural areas. The extent of relative poverty is at its most conspicuous in the urban areas, where the very rich and the very poor live side by side. Vandalism of community infrastructure by alienated youth is costly to the poor living in the urban slums. Drug and alcohol abuse, AIDS, domestic violence, female depression and family breakdown, though not the exclusive domain of urban poverty, are nevertheless a widespread urban phenomenon.[8]

The fourth set of problems arise from the interventions of the State. The urban poor have more contact with the agencies of the State. Many poor perceive and experience the State in negative ways. An oppressive bureaucracy which attempts to regulate the urban poor without understanding their problems, and a corrupt policeman, demanding money for turning a blind eye to illegal income generating activities, are typical examples.[9] Planners often have little understanding about how the urban poor survive.[10]

We have very briefly summarised the main problems of the urban poor into four clusters. They are, however, inter-connected. They are not also exclusive to the urban poor only. They may be present in rural areas as well. It is not necessary that all the problems are necessarily present in urban areas at once all the time. What we need to recognise is that in urban areas these problems appear in such unique combinations that they intensify the insecurity, the life-threatening health risks associated with poverty and influence the coping startegies adopted by the poor at the household and community levels.[11]

Let us now see how far our Chamar Tolla conforms to this scheme of problems.

Social tension emanating from a conflict of individual interest with communal interest, and the art of "one-upmanship", characterised the Tolla life.

Lack of approach roads and village lanes bothered our inhabitants, just as their brethren in the urban areas found them as basic necessities. Drainage and sanitation were high on their problem tree, just as they are in urban slums.

Unemployment was a problem : it was the eighth most important problem in a bundle of only a dozen problems. This is a characteristic of urban slums as well, where everyone has some employment though not fully employed throughout the year.

Housing is seldom stated up-front in rural areas as a major cause for concern, but it was indeed a problem for the inhabitants of our Chamar Tolla, like a typical urban habitat.

Educational facilities is last in the list of priorities, a situation scarcely found in rural areas, after the increase in the reach of the media and the literacy mission campaigns unleashed by the State.

What distinguishes the rural slum from a typical urban slum is that the causes that generate some of these problems are different. For instance internal conflicts and lack of unity amongst the inhabitants of our Chamar Tolla reflected a degenerated social environment. But unlike in an urban slum, disturbed social environment was not caused by social diversity, differences in lifestyles of people with existence of very rich and very poor concurrently, vandalism of community infrastructure (howsoever meagre), drug abuse, alcoholism, dominance perpetrated by lumpen elements and communalism. The disturbed social environment in the Chamar Tolla was a result of strategic behaviour of the inhabitants, placed at a great disadvantage in dealing with the onslaught of the both man and nature, in which there is a conflict of individual interest with community's interest, and the art of "one-upmanship". Each trying to have what he barely needs from the same "cake" where the "cake" is desperately small.

Similarly, the problem of "landlessness" conveys a different meaning in the context of the rural slum. In most urban slums, the inhabitants have no title to their homestead land, and the slum dwellers in urban areas do not seek non-homestead land because the nature of their employment is casual labour, petty trading etc. which do not need land as a factor of production. In case of the rural slum, the slum dwellers have right, title and possession of their hutments, but seek land for cultivation because off-farm employment opportunities like casual labour, petty trading etc., are virtually non-existent. Interestingly, a crucial difference follows from this. Whereas in urban slums the dwellers have no *patta,* but have several other facilities and gadgets: water, electricity (sometimes illegally), refrigerator, television and the like, though not everyone has all of them all the time. The rural dwellers have *patta* for their land, but have none of the gadgets and facilities: no electricity, no water, no refrigerator, no television.

Consider next the problem of drainage and sanitation. Normally in rural areas the "right to drain" water is taken for granted and it is fairly common to allow used water to flow freely in fallow lands and/or fields adjoining human settlements without demur or recourse. And the water so discharged into adjoining fields and fallow land is absorbed fairly quickly or they flow further down and in some cases eventually to a *nulla* or rivulet. One therefore, seldom, if at all, gets to notice the problems of drainage in rural setting except in the limiting cases of floods and "flood-like situations". In urban slums, the absence of drainage facilities or their overuse/misuse, are the underlying problems. In our Chamar Tolla, however, the problem was that the upper caste farmers, who owned lands around the Chamar Tolla were in no mood to allow their land to be used for draining water (used or otherwise) accumulated around the hutments. It was not a case of caste politics/ caste-conflicts or untouchability, if you like. It is just the anti-altruistic feeling of not allowing "our-land" to be used for any purpose which does not entail (at least in the short-run) any direct benefit to "us", the land-owners. They were not even ready to allow drainage for a "fee".

In the matter of unemployment, the rural slum dwellers are not confronted with problems of casualisation, unfair rewards, informal nature of their engagement, commoditization process and increasing commercialisation. Their problem was they simply had no job. Chamars are traditionally cobblers. The advent of plastic shoes and the availability of ready made shoes in the nearby markets, have diminished the scope of the Chamars in earning their livelihoods, Secondly by law they can no longer deal with hides of dead domestic animals which gave them some income to ecke out a living. Thus the problem of unemployment was one of no work at all. It is open unemployment. Since the inhabitants of our Chamar Tolla had no agricultural lands, there was no question of any disguised unemployment as well.

Conclusions

Slums can, therefore, occur either in rural or urban landscapes. The problems of these slums may appear to be similar at first sight. But the underpinning cause of the seemingly similar set of problems may be different for rural and urban areas. The solutions to the problems would, thus be different. Since we did not necessarily "bargained" (not an appropriate word) a detailed problem solving exercise, we do not wish to comment on it further. It is a limitation of this study. We would return to Saddopur some day to do so.

Acknowledgements

I would like to thank: (i) the villagers of Chamar Tolla, Saddopur Village, Ghazipur District, for sharing their knowledge with us and no less for their hospitality and kindness; (ii) Dr. Sarojini Fernando, Director, BUDS, Bangalore for her comments; and (iii) the facilitators, whose names are mentioned in the diagrammes for their help. The responsibility for the errors are solely mine.

NOTES

1. Idris Jazairy *et al., The State of World Rural Poverty* (Rome: International Fund for Agricultural Development) 1995.
2. David Harvey, *Social Justice and the City* (London: Edwar Arnold), 1975.
3. Trudy Harpham, Tim Lusty and Patrick Vaughan (eds.): *In the Shadow of the City: Community Health and the Urban Poor* (Oxford and New York: Oxford University Press) 1988. Charles Surjadi : "Respiratory Diseases of Mothers and Children and Environmental Factors among Households in Jakarta", in *Environment and Urbanisation,* Vol. 5, No. 2, pp. 78-86, 1993. I. Tabibzadeh, A. Rossi Espagnet and R. Maxwell: *Spotlight on the Cities: Improving Urban Health in Developing Countries* (Geneva: World Health Organisation) 1989.
4. Jane Pryer and Nigel Crook: *Cities of Hunger: Urban Malnutrition in Developing Countries* (Oxford: Oxfam) 1988.
5. John Harris: "Urban poverty and Urban Poverty Alleviation", *Cities.* August, 1989.
6. Irma Adelman and Cynthia Taft Morris: "Growth and Impoverishment in the Middle of the Nineteenth Century", in *World Development,* Vol. 6, No. 3, 1978, pp.245-273.
7. Jo Boyden: *Children of the Cities* (London: Zed) 1991. Gilberto Dimenstein: *Brazil: War on Children* (London: Latin American Bureau) 1991.
8. Ellen Wratten: "Conceptualising Urban Poverty" in *Environment and Urbanisation,* Vol. 7, No. 1, 1995.
9. Nici Nelson: "How Women and Men Get By: the Sexual Division of Labour in a Squatter Settlement" in Joseph Gugler (ed.): *The Urbanisation of the Third World* (Oxford: Oxford University Press) 1988.
10. Carole Rakodi: "Planning for Whom?" in Nick Devas and Carole Rakodi (eds.): Managing Fast Growing Cities: *New Approaches to Urban Planning and Management in the Developing World* (Harlow: Longman) 1993.
11. *Ibid.*

9

COMMUNITY DEVELOPMENT IN INDONESIA

Some Lessons for India

— VINITA KUMAR

Introduction

A recent visit to Indonesia sponsored by the UNICEF revealed that though the country has a lot in common with India, there are vital differences especially with regard to the approach to community development. Both India and Indonesia shared a colonial past and got their independence within two years of each other. At the time of Independence both the countries were basically agrarian and faced with the problem of food shortage, poverty, rising population and limited resources for development. Both embarked on a series of five year plans aimed at developing the economy. However, whereas India laid emphasis on physical capital accumulation and building up of an industrial base for the future growth of the economy, in Indonesia there was a relatively greater emphasis on human resource development and building up community institutions and cadres for delivery of social goods.

During the First Long Term Development Period (PJP I, 1969/70—1993/94) which ended with the completion of the Fifth Five Development Plan (Replita V, 1989/90—1993-94), rural development formed an integral part of national planning for Indonesia. The implementation of village development activities were executed through several special programmes which aimed at creating village development special funds, improving and guidance of Work Area Development Unit (Unit Daerah Kejra Pambangungan/UDPK), increasing self-sustained village communities and family welfare guidance. A description of some of the important programmes/experiences in community development in Indonesia is given below with the aim of deriving useful lessons for India.

PROGRAMMES FOR HUMAN DEVELOPMENT IN THE COMMUNITY

Health, Family Welfare and Population Control

Concern about the rapid population growth and its implications on health and family welfare began as early as in 1957 when a group of concerned community leaders established the Indonesian Planned Parenthood Association. The year 1970 marked the beginning of the Government commitment to take tangible steps to control the population growth and at the same time to enhance the welfare status of the people. It was in that year that the National Family Planning Coordinating Board (BKKBN) was established with the explicit mandate to coordinate all family planning activities undertaken by all government and non-government agencies. In 1976 BKKBN launched the Village Family Planning Programme to make family planning services accessible throughout the country including the remote parts.

In the beginning the BKKBN established the Village Contraceptive Distribution Centres (VCDC) manned by volunteer cadres whose role was merely to distribute supplies, do motivational work and to maintain village family planning records. The emphasis was not on the appointment of volunteer cadres but on establishing the network and the institution within the village community structure.

In 1979 the Integrated Health and Family Planning Programme later known as the POSYANDU was launched. The Posyandu is an acronym for 'Post for Integrated Services'. This is a collection of Integrated and coordinated health, family planning and other social services provided by the community for the community itself. It is conducted once each month. The programme has multiple aims primary amongst which are reducing fertility and infant mortality rates. The services provided include resupply and follow up checks for continuing contraceptive uses, simple health treatment, immunization, weighting of children under five for growth monitoring, food supplementation, nutrition enrollment, practical oral rehydration therapy and also provision of social information and education.

The Posyandu is also a forum of communication in which other community development issues e.g. economic, political and villages are conveyed and discussed. In village Susukan, in Banjarnegara district of Central Java, we saw a Posyandu in operation. Women had turned up in great numbers along with the children. Each was dressed as if for a special occasion. There was a general atmosphere of festivity. One got the impression that Posyandu are social meetings as well where mothers gather to chat and exchange news. This is an important departure from the clinical approach to health and family welfare resulting in greater participation by the community.

Each village usually has one Posyandu serving approximately 120 households and 100 children under 5 depending upon availability of personnel for the Posyandu and upon the situation in the area. Throughout Indonesia there are approximately 200,000 Posyandu held every month.

There is an in-built system of incentives and reward for those practicing family planning methods. The peer pressure to practice family planning is also high. Not only is there religious sanction but also religious approbation for limiting the size of the family for welfare reasons. Since religion has a fairly important place in people's life in villages, this has also exercised a positive influence on acceptance of family planning. It would have a direct bearing on the welfare of women who are the cutting edge of family planning strategies. The Family Welfare Income Generating Activities was started for family planing acceptors. At the beginning this scheme was to provide monetary incentives and rewards to continuing contraceptive users and to encourage them to form acceptor groups that could give "peer pressure" to other village members. As these groups became viable village institutions and as they acquired the managerial skills in handling revolving funds, BKKBN graduated these groups to become Family Welfare Groups with access to considerably bigger loans. The effective convergence of income generating schemes with family planning has been another important and successful experiment in Indonesia from which lessons can be drawn for other developing countries.

Family Welfare Movement (PKK)

The implementation of family welfare programmes was also helped by the Family Welfare Movement (PKK) which is an organisation originally established to expand the role of women beyond the traditional limited household and child bearing role. Initially emphasising income generation, it was later expanded to raise the awareness of women in educational, economic and social, political and cultural matters.

The PKK has been an important force in the dissemination of family planning information and motivation, particularly in remote areas where other community organisations are rudimentary. The PKK has established a number of cadres at the village level to assist with family planning and other work. At present there are approximately 2 million PKK volunteers actively involve in grass-root level of social development. For the family planning the most important is the Posyandu cadre which assumes the bulk of the responsibility to organise and implement the community Posyandus. The PKK has been receiving Rupaya 500,000 per village per year from the Presidential assistance fund.

Bina Kelvarga Dan Balita (BKB) is a family and child development programme aimed at improving the knowledge, attitudes and skills of village mothers on how to raise their infants and children. The target group for this programme consists of mothers having a child or children under five years living near the BKB centre who are actively participating in Posyandu activities and are also family planning acceptors. To support this activity one cadre is trained for every 25 mothers. The cadre then conducts a 16 meeting educational programme for the other mothers. Cadres are provided with sets of educational toys. The content of the training programme consists of information on BKB programme in general, physical and mental development of the child, physical motoric and sensory motoric development of the child, language and intellectual development, self-reliance and problem solving abilities.

Both the PKK and the BKB have made effective use of Information, Education and Communication (IEC) strategies for bringing about general awareness, knowledge about programmes and services, closer networking and personal touch with cadres and government officials, and change in attitudes. The frequent interactions of the motivators/facilitators/cadres/field workers with the target group has resulted in a " two-way" communication of message, i.e., from the Government to the people and from the people to the government.

Education

Realisation of the importance of education as a means of development came fairly early in the planning process. Education in Indonesia is not conceived in the narrow sense of increasing the literacy rate but as a means of strengthening the nation through developing its people to have faith in God, to have knowledge and skills, to be self reliant and to have an understanding of the social and national responsibilities. Religious values and nationalism are imbued very early in school life and Islamic scriptures and Pancila form an integral part of the school curriculum till High School. This approach holds some important lessons for India where education is confined to classrooms and in text books with little relevance to values of society and life in general. Education should be viewed much more than being able to read and write one's name. At the primary education level a conscious effort should be made to imbue the child with national values and give a grounding in the code of conduct which the society wants from each individual. The power of education/Literacy Campaign in getting rid of a social evil and enforcing a particular code of conduct is evident from experiment in Andhra Pradesh. This experiment has been done on a much large scale in Indonesia.

The Universal Six-years Primary Education Programme was the most important programme in PJP I resulting in an increase in the enrolment rates of school aged children in the seven to twelve years age bracket. This being followed by the Nine-year Basic Educational Programme in PJP II which aims at making basic education available to everybody, including children living in remote areas. The programme envisages gradual abolition of school fees, abolition of requirements for entering middle school and introduction of scholarships for outstanding students belonging to deprived sections. By the end of PJP-I almost all of the school aged children were enrolled in six-year primary schools compared to only 41.4 per cent in 1968-69. In addition, the illiteracy rate of the population aged 10 years and older has continued to fall from 39.1 per cent at the start of PTP-I to only 15.8 per cent in 1990.

The Non-formal Education is another important aspect of the education system in Indonesia which has relevance for India. This programme focuses on literacy in the Indonesian national language, simple arithmetic and basic knowledge and skills to improve living standards. Learning activities are implemented through learning groups consisting mostly of women who are taught by volunteer tutors. These groups are later provided revolving loan funds for income generating activities. The stress on education of women has been one of the key factors in reducing the total fertility rates and bringing about improvement in various health indicators. Besides this, the convergence of non-formal education with employment/income generating activities not only lends credibility to this education programme but is expected to lead to better handling of assistance/loan through basic knowledge in arithmetic/accounting and acquisition of basic knowledge and skills.

Poverty Alleviation

The Inpres Desa Tertinggal (IDT) also known as Presidential Instruction on Poverty Alleviation Programme was started with the aim of promoting efforts for alleviating poverty in less developed villages in a sustainable manner. Through this programme sectoral and regional programmes are encouraged in such a manner so as to appraise needs of poor villages to arrive at results which will have a significant impact on alleviation of poverty. The three major inputs of the IDT programme are:

(i) providing facilities in the poor villages,
(ii) providing funds for socio-economic activities, and
(iii) providing basic physical and social infrastructure.

The less developed village is defined and identified by the State Ministers for National Development Planning/Chairman of the National Development Planning Agency and the Minister of Home Affairs on the basis of data resulting from a sectoral bureau of Statistics Survey. A community group is formed consisting of farm labourers, peasants etc, categorised as poor. The IDT Programme provides special assistance in the form of working capital with guidance and technical assistance for opening up business opportunities.

A total of US $ 10 million have been allocated per village to a little over 20 thousand IDT Village throughout the country. IDT groups in the villages get approximately the equivalent of Rs. 5000 per person for group activities such as cattle fattening, house building, provision of basic sanitation facilities etc.

The experience of poverty alleviation in Indonesia has been commendable manifesting itself in expansion of employment opportunities, which in conjunction with a falling population growth rate, has resulted in the continued increase in the standard of living of the Indonesian people. Income per capita, which in 1969 was around US $ 70 rose to approximately US $ 700 by 1993-94 and is currently more than US $ 900. Meanwhile, the number of people living below the official poverty line dropped drastically. While in 1970 there were 70 million poor people in the country accounting for 60 per cent of the population, by 1993 this number has dropped to 25.9 million people or 13.7 of the entire population.

THE DELIVERY MECHANISMS FOR COMMUNITY DEVELOPMENT

The reduction in level of poverty and improvement in the quality of life in rural areas owes much to the type of institutions and delivery systems existing at the village level and their effectiveness in delivering social goods. There are several similarities in the administrative structures of Indonesia and India, specially in the sense that the power flows from the top to the bottom. However, Indonesia has evolved several alternative mechanisms rooted in the community which has facilitated a bottom up approach essential for the success of the above mentioned schemes. A description of some of the top down and the bottom up mechanisms is given below.

Administrative Set-up

There is a well defined structure of Government exercising a direct line of control over various functions which has helped in streamlining the community delivery systems in Indonesia. The President and the Vice-President appoint the Ministers in-charge of various Ministries and Departments, the Attorney General, the commander of Armed Forces and the Central Bank and special changes. The President also directly appoints the Governor of Provinces and autonomous regions as well as the provincial council. At the district level, the Bhupati is the head of the district/muncipality which is an appointee of the Governor and is often from the Army. All the sub-district officials are directly responsible to the Bhupati and can be appointed/dismissed by him if need be. However, dismissals are rare and the government officials have a tenure of posting of at least five years giving them ample opportunity to devote their attention to development of the district/ the sub-district/the village. A direct line of control is established with the president of the country as the head of the nation, the Bhupati is heading the districts, the Camat heading the sub-districts and the Kapala Desa heading the village. This highly structured administrative setup working in a unitary system of government with almost non-existant opposition has facilitated delivery of social goods in a streamlined manner. This is further facilitated through a strong feeling of nationalism, respect for authority and a value system wherein debate, dissent and voicing of disagreement is frowned upon by the society and consent and consensus are the order of the day.

Local Self Government

According to the Republic of Indonesia Act (1979), the village is the lowest government organisation structure headed by the sub-district Chairman of the Camat having the right to organise its own internal affairs under the integrity and unity of the Republic of Indonesia. The Lembaga Ketahan Masyarakat Desa (LKMD) or the Village Resilience Community Institution could be likened to the village Panchayat in India with the Kepala Desa (the equivalent of Sarpanch) being an elected member for five years. The last level of administration is the hamlet/Community Association (RW)/Neighbourhood Association (RT). (The village communities have the tradition of discussing issues (Musyawarah) and arriving at mutual understanding (Gotong Royong) on solutions to various problems facing the community. This is facilitated through creation of awareness through IEC, trained and committed cadre of workers, committed NGOs and support of religious leaders.

The LKMD functions as a deliberative forum to energise, foster and develop the economic endeavours of the community and to select various support activities from governmental agencies and institutions as well as from the private sector. The LKMD collects all activity proposals from poor families through community groups. The approach is to implant feelings of comradeship and encourage mutual cooperation, while emphasising activities based on self-reliance. The members of the target community are involved in the decision making process from the very early stages of planning, through implementation and upto achievement of results.

The LKMD is the equivalent of the *Gram Panchayat* and the *Gram Sabha* in India. Experience in Indonesia has shown the LKMD to be the focal point of all development activities at the village level. The meetings organised in the Community Hall (equivalent of *Panchayat Ghar*) by the LKMD of respective villages were well attended showing the interest of the community in the various activities. We were also impressed by the awareness of the people of various important issues during the "question-answer" sessions during these meetings. Equally impressive was the participation of women in these meetings. Despite a few giggles and some sniggers they did not hesitate to discuss the kind of family planning they were practicing.

Cadres and Other Field Staff

A central factor in the success of community development schemes in Indonesia is the existence of voluntary village development workers or cadres who become the link between the activated organiser and the target community. These cadres consist of mainly women. The cadres have a distinct identity which is brought out by different colour uniforms worn by them. Most cadres are voluntary and do not accept payment. We were interested in finding out the reason for the high level of motivation among them despite the fact that theirs is not a paid job. The impression one got was that being enrolled in a cadre was some kind of a prestige issue which was rooted in the values of the society. This was also related to the esteem attached to helping others/doing social work to create a just and equal society under the precepts of Islam. The women enlisted in the cadres probably belonged to the economically better off strata and, therefore, did not require remuneration in terms of money.

Training is an important instrument in building up cadres. A description of the Posyandu cadres has already been given in one of the earlier sections. Regency Health Staff, Community Health Centres, doctors, district heads and their staff, village leaders and community leaders in general were some of the others targeted in formal and informal training activities. Using this approach PPSE and the Regency Health Service have been able to create awareness amongst key people at various levels of local government and thus increase the reach of activities and the transfer of knowledge.

In addition to volunteers and social workers who may work on a self supporting and voluntary basis, technical facilitators are also recruited from field workers at the sub-district and village levels from various departments and social organisations such as the Department of Home Affairs (Trainers on Integrated Village Development/LPDT), Department of Agriculture (Agricultural Field Worker Assistance Specialists/PPL and PPS), Department of Social Affairs (Sub-district Social Affairs Officers/PSK), Karang Taruna (Neighbourhood Youth Association), etc.

The women have an important role to play in the formation of cadres. This is probably in recognition of the fact that the women are more sensitive to the needs of children, and that of the community at large. The Dharma Wanitas are entirely women cadres, consisting of the wife of the Bhupati and her counterparts at various levels, i.e., the Chamat, the Kapala Desa, etc., as women representatives at various levels. Some of these women are very active participants in meetings of the community to discuss problems. One should also not discount a keen sense of competition among cadres to excel themselves. This is promoted through giving of a distinct identity in terms of a name and a uniform as well as a motto and a slogan. There is also the practice of ranking the villages and districts in terms of performance which further promotes a keen sense of competition among them. Not only is the status of workers elevated in society on account of social work but there is also a strong spirit of togetherness and comaraderie among the workers and the community. This is further strengthened by organisation of get-togethers and singing of songs which have a message for community development. The "Posyandu" songs and songs embodying the principles of Pancila are quite well known, popular and sung even by the smallest children.

Role of Religious Leaders

The positive use of religion in the Indonesian society and polity again holds very important lessons for India. Religion has not only played a role in moulding the minds of the people but has been used by the state for making communities accept national policies. From the beginning care was taken to involve the leaders of various religious communities in positive interpretation of these policies. There is a separate Ministry of Religious Affairs to provide the necessary interface between the Government and the communities on religious matters. Given the elaborate network that most religions have for reaching communities, this has been effectively mobilised for not only disseminating awareness about government policies and programmes but also making communities realise the benefits of this in the larger interest of the whole society.

As already mentioned, Islam has been used positively and pragmatically for spreading the message of family planning. The Muhammadiyah and the Nandlatul Ulama Family Welfare Unit provide IEC through Islamic religious activities and services through Islamic medical facilities. Similarly, the Indonesian Council of Churches provides similar facilities to communities through churches. The religious leaders with the advantage of reaching communities on a rather intimate level and relating subjects to "righteous living" have played an important role in Indonesia's community development. Though most religions believe that children are a gift of God, the religious leaders advocate that it is the welfare of children which is also the prime responsibility of the parents. Hence it is not just the birth but the nurturing of children which has acquired a greater significance in the minds of the people helping the family planners to advocate birth control. The giving away of alms is also advocated as an essential principle of Islam which has resulted in voluntary services to the society by a large number of people including those working in cadres. Tolerance to other religions, patience, endurance, frugality in existence and spartan existence are some of the other religious values that has helped in nurturing responsible and tolerant religious communities co-existing peacefully.

INDICATORS OF HUMAN DEVELOPMENT

As a result of the above mentioned programmes, the institutions and effective delivery mechanisms described above, the health and nutrition condition of the population has continued to improve. Life expectancy in Indonesia has increased from 45.7 years in 1967 to 62.7 years by the end of PJP-I. In the same period the infant mortality rate has decreased from 145 to 58 per thousand life births. Calorie intake has increased from 20 to 35 calories per capita per day in 1968 to 2701 calories per capita per day in 1990 and this has been accompanied by increased consumption of protein and other nutrients.

COMMUNITY PARTICIPATION IN DEVELOPMENT

The Kring

A very notable feature of community development in Indonesia is the extent and quality of community participation. The Kring is a case in point. A description of a Kring session which took place late in the evening of 11 October 1995 in village Tempuran in the district of Banjarnegara (Central Java) and lasted for more than three hours gave useful insights into how the community is drawn to discuss the various problems confronting it and encouraged to find solutions for these.

The genesis of the Kring lies in the Banjarnegara Primary Health Care programme which was designed with the objective of improving community welfare through appropriate programmes which activated community participation. The programme had three major components:

(i) Participation in those activities which reflect the real needs of the people,

(ii) Working through existing community structure, and
(iii) Building up complementarity with the broader regency development programmes.

This was in realisation of the fact that only when the target community feels that the programme belongs to them that they fully and enthusiastically participate in it. The approach was, therefore, based on the principle that the community must have access to information relevant to their needs. The media utilised for this transfer of knowledge included informal interaction and communication, trainees for voluntary village development workers (Cadres) and village and district officials, orientation for District Heads and regency officials, and advocacy of policy to those in position of authority. The goal of this approach is that the combination of such communication will create dynamics within the community which will gradually attain a critical memorandum so that development will become an accepted and natural part of community life.

The Banjarnegara Health Programme started off in just a few villages located in one district but gradually spread to cover the whole of the regency. This dissemination of the programme was able to occur partly because of the enthusiasm of NGOs and Government officials but primarily due to increased awareness of the community and their desire to participate in community development programmes.

During the 1980s while PPSE's activities were diversified to cover such fields as group credit programmes, toilet construction, Consultations etc. A uniformly development planning forum known as Kring was developed where a number of villages were grouped into a forum to be utilised to assist in the resolution of problems facing the community. Through regular Workshops involving up to 10 village in any one district the Kring system creates an atmosphere of inter-village solidarity as village representatives share the experience and seek possible solutions to the problems confronted by their communities. The emphasis at the Workshop is transfer of knowledge to key people to the community in order that they can then take a measure of responsibility for community development activities in their own regions.

The Kring programme has been dynamic one and has changed its emphasis over the years according to the needs of the community at any particular time. After the initial focus on the malaria problem, Kring became more general in nature giving greater emphasis to overcoming serious health problems faced by the community and taking on a more general developmental emphasis thus evolving into village community Development Kring. This transition arose as a result of the meeting held between Government officials including the Bhupati, YPPSE and other concerned parties in which it was decided that Kring had great potential as a tool to assist in the formulation of village development plans by transfer knowledge and about general community development principles to decision makers and others at the village level. The prime aim of PMD Kring is to functionalise the village LKMD by providing its members with inputs both from the community and from above and by providing technical support through the Kring Forum. Currently they are both pre-Kring and Post-Kring workshops. Pre-Kring workshops are designed to enable villages to prepare the material they will take to the district level Kring Workshops while post-Kring functions as a review of the results of the latter workshops. Thus two village level workshops are attended by a wide variety of participants such as village Heads in formal and informal community leaders, neighbourhood Heads, cadres and LKMD. This means that all participants are treated as equals. No matter what their status is in the community, inputs are expected from all participants and not just community leaders. Those who attend the Kring Workshops includes District Heads, Health Centre doctors and staff, LKMD leaders, cadres, village Heads, informal leaders and YPPSE staff.

The KRING session organised by volunteers of YPPSE met on October 11, 1995 at village Tempuran to approach the problems of community development with the villagers. At the beginning of the session the Kapaladesa listed out the annual budget of the village and the achievement against the physical and financial targets. Against each project the basic problems in implementation were also discussed. As a result of these discussions the following difficulties/problems were listed:

1. Health

Under this category the following problems were identified :

1. Shortage of latrines,
2. Location of community toilets,
3. Shortage of clean water, and
4. Environment.

2. Education

1. Shortage of staff, and
2. Shortage of furniture.

3. Farming

1. Low price of vegetables.
2. High price of fertiliser,
3. Problem of pests, and
4. Disease of the root.

4. Animal Husbandry

1. Lack of green fodder,
2. Low price of chicken,
3. High price of feed, and
4. Disease.

5. Mental Problems

Small size of mosque

Against each of these problems the solutions were discussed with the participants. It was pointed out that shortage of latrines could be related to lack of knowledge/awareness about healthy life and the low priority given to these by individuals. The problem of finding location for community latrine also emanated from the low priority given to this item in the village community. This could also partly be related to lack of water and the problem of bringing water supplied from the local spring. The storage of water in small tanks for common use for purposes of drinking, washing, bathing etc. also pose a health problem. The proposal of giving basins on credit was mooted and it was decided that this proposal could be discussed in smaller meetings. Findings new sources of water was also proposed.

Farming

It was pointed out that the problems under farming basically resulted from over supply of cabbage. It was suggested that the farmers adopt mix cropping and intercropping and change the root of crops for better fertility of soil as well as for taking care of the problem of low price of cabbage. Animal fertilisers supplemented by planning acacia plant could fix the nitrogen in the soil and thereby improve its fertility. It was also pointed out that the cost of root disease has often resulted in planting the same crop every year. Leaving part of the land fallow could solve this problem.

The interesting feature of the KRING session was utilisation of the discussion not only for identifying the problems of the village and difficulties faced in implementation of ongoing schemes but also framing a knowledge base for formulating projects for the next year with the 'right' priorities. Two main proposals for the next year which emerged from the discussion were: (i) laying of three km. pipe from the forest to the village for purposes of drinking water, (ii) Problem of latrine and waste disposal were also accorded greater priority during the next Plan.

The Mawas Diri Project

Another instance of active community participation was witnessed in the Community based Environmental Sanitation Programme in Boyalali District. The Yayasan Indonesia Sejahtera (YIS) with the help of funds from the International Fund for Agricultural Development (IFAD) has tried to develop an integrated community health programme participatory action technique in two sub-districts in rural areas and one urban ward. The basic objective of this project is to increase community health status by increasing basic sanitation. This is done through involvement and strengthening of local institutions related with community health and sanitation activities and developing a community development model . Under the Mawas Diri Project people are encouraged to assess. discuss and solve their sanitation problems in a simple, practical and educative way. A Revolving Fund is created consisting of Rp. 2 million for one group of families. One village can have a maximum of 3 to 5 groups. The implementor institution at the village level are LKMD and RT at the sub-village level. The repayment from the RT must be saved at the sub-district bank in the name of the LKMD representative. The saving account is held in the name of the Kapala Desa. The interest rate for credit to the member is decided by the group.

In the Siswodipuran and the Karanggeneng village of Boyalali district in Central Java we visited the Mawas Diri Project on the 16th of October 1995. In the YIS office at Solo we were familiarised with the survey of households conducted at the RT level in which details about the house in terms of lighting, air circulation, floor, water waste, fence stable, clean water, water closet, drinking water were categorised as "good" or "bad". The availability/non-availability of the above mentioned facilities were discussed with the groups. The self-survey helped arrive at priorities of the households regarding their felt needs about physical facilities which had a direct bearing on environmental sanitation. The groups consisting of 30 to 40 members were made aware about the importance of sanitation, waste disposal, design of houses, etc. through meetings conducted by the LKMD and YIS. Once the members decided on their priorities, they were given access to the revolving fund and also required to contribute 50 per cent of the project cost. The duration of the credit was 24 months and the rate of interest charged was 1 per cent per month of which 0.75 per cent is for the group and 0.25 per cent is for the LKMD. The sub-district official was made responsible for monitoring, supervising and administering the programme, the Puskesmas staff was responsible for sanitation and technical support and YIS was responsible for human resource development and strengthening the management aspect of the programme.

A number of households visited under the project had opted to get the floor of the house cemented even though supply of clean water was perhaps a more important need. The reason why a higher individual priority was given to cementing of floor was more for "aesthetic" value rather than sanitation requirement. Some of the households had, nevertheless opted for construction of a WC and a water tank which had greater relevance for health. However, the fact that the project was undertaken by the members strictly in terms of their felt needs and requirements and not imposed from the "top" was a good starting point. All the group members were able to repay the loan and there was no case of default.

Village/Family Level Data Base

The village visited had an impressive data base. The community Halls where formal meetings took place with the officials and the residents of the village had a detailed "Papan Monograph Desa" on the wall containing information about the demographic characteristics (Population by sex, age, occupation), social indicators such as number of schools, literacy rate, number of children attending school, sanitation status reflected in number of households having latrines, etc. Even more impressive were the kind of data collected in the "neighbourhood lists" or RT. The Peta Keluarga Sejahtera (PKS) or the Family Welfare Map seen by us listed adult women in 46 households by the following categories: (i) those using contraceptives, (ii) those not using contraceptives, and (iii) those who have reached menopause. The first category was further broken down into the type of family planning practiced, viz., (a) those using IUD, (b) those using pills, (c) those taking injections. Pregnant women were identified separately.

Besides indicators of family planning, the PKS also had details of the level of prosperity of the households. A nation-wide Census of families is conducted to identify five stages of Family Welfare Development. The Pre-Welfare stage is one where families have no capabilities to meet their basic human needs for food, clothing and shelter. To identify such families the following criteria are used:

(i) do family members follow the teaching of religion,
(ii) have two meals a day,
(iii) have three sets of clothes,
(iv) have at least two-thirds of floor area of the house cemented, and
(v) had a sick member who availed of medical facilities.

Households not meeting the above five criteria are classified as less prosperous or belonging to Pre-welfare stage. The next level of prosperity or Welfare Stage I includes those families which are capable of meeting the above criteria. Welfare Stage II is one where physical human needs are met but not the psychological, family planning needs. The indicators used for identifying such families are as follows:

(i) Do all members of the family pray 5 times a day,
(ii) have a diet which includes animal protein at least once a week,
(iii) buy new clothes every year,
(iv) have floor space of at least 8 sq.metres per member,
(v) had incidence of sickness during the previous 3 months due to which the person could not go for regular work,
(vi) have at least one member in the household with more than 15 days of stable income,
(vii) have all literate members in the household,
(viii) have all children in the age group 6 to 15 years attending school, and
(ix) have all eligible members practicing family planning after having a minimum of two children,

Welfare Stage III include seven more criteria to identify those families capable of meeting both physical and psychological needs but not in a position to meet developmental needs such as savings and information. The Census lists out

(i) Families making special effort to acquire religious knowledge,
(ii) Families having savings,
(iii) Families sitting together for meal at least once during the day,
(iv) Families having community involvement,
(v) Families able to have recreation at least one in six months,
(vi) Families having access to radio, T.V., magazine, etc., and
(vii) Families possessing own vehicle (cycle, motor cycle, etc.)

The Fourth Level of Prosperity or Welfare Stage III + is defined as that stage of prosperity where families are capable of meeting all physical, psychological and developmental needs but are not able to contribute to community activities. In addition to the criteria mentioned above

(i) Families where at least one member has the ability to give donations, alms, etc.
(ii) Families where at least one member is actively involved in community welfare through organisations/institutions, etc.

are included in this final Welfare Stage III +. It is interesting to note that the level of prosperity is related to religion and the ability of the family to contribute to the community besides physical indicators such as food, floor space, clothing, etc. The impressive data base available at the household level in village communities has made it possible to plan welfare activities in consonance with the needs of the people.

COMMUNITY DEVELOPMENT IN INDIA AND INDONESIA : SOME COMPARISONS

Though both India and Indonesia shared common problems of development at the time of their Independence, the two countries have evolved quite differently over the last twenty-five years or so. The reason for this partly lies in Indonesia's oil reserves (when India was reeling under foreign exchange crisis during the seventies on account of escalation in oil prices, Indonesia had surplus funds which could be utilised for developmental purposes), the unitary form of Government, political stability and economic reforms as early as the eighties. Though these factors have been important, perhaps more significant has been the difference in the perception of the two countries on how to tackle the problem of poverty.

India's initial years of planning laid great emphasis on physical capital accumulation, industrialisation and building of basic infrastructure in the hope that growth would ultimately help the community at large. When growth failed to pick up significantly and poverty did not show any declining trend during the sixties and the seventies, the Government of India turned to direct poverty alleviation programmes particularly those geared to creation of wage and self employment. During the same period the Government of Indonesia adopted a totally different developmental strategy and concentrated upon human resource and community development through health and family welfare, population control and education. Whereas India was struggling during the sixties and the seventies to build cooperatives, expand bank branches in rural areas, open District Industrial Centres, establish Small Farmers Development Agency, etc. to deliver productive physical inputs to the disadvantaged, Indonesia was building cadres to deliver social goods such as health, education, family welfare, etc. to the people.

The second major point of departure is with respect to empowerment of the people at the grass-root level. It is ironical that India with its dream of community development and Panchayati Raj inspired by Mahatma Gandhi with the aim of bringing about a prosperity and self reliance at the village level was an ideology which could not be translated into action. A beginning was made in the Community Development Programme during the sixties but this did not make much headway. In contrast to the Indian experience, Indonesia seems to have succeeded to a much larger extent in empowering the LKMD or the Village Resilience Community Institution. This institution is quite active in planning and executing projects in consonance with the needs of the community. The vibrancy of the LKMD can be guaged by the frequency of the meetings arranged and the impressive turnout of the community members. This indicates the confidence the community imposes on the LKMD as an effective body in sorting out issues and problems. The spirit of "Musyarwara and the practice of "Gotongryong" or arrival at solutions and mutual consent through discussions is a tradition which has been kept alive in community meetings.

The third area of difference lies in the changing values of the community in the two countries. Before Independence the aim of getting rid of foreign rule had united Indian communities and made them come together with a common vision and goal. However, with the achievement of Independence, sharp communal divisions emerged on the lines of religion, politics, caste, creed, etc. Furthermore, with growing income inequalities, high levels of poverty in rural areas, and growing ineffectiveness of village level institutions, decay in basic values set in. There was also a spawning of a multitude of political parties each with different ideologies dividing communities further on party lines.

In contrast, Indonesia with a single party system, political stability and virtually no opposition to the President had very favourable conditions for unifying various ethnic communities under a strong Central leadership. A strong sense of nationalism brought through propagation of the Pancila advocating belief in one supreme God, a just and civilised society, unity among all, democracy and social justice has imbued the people with a strong sense of values. The village communities are by and large cut-off from outside influences partly because of state controlled media and limited knowledge of languages other than Bahasa Indonesia. This could be instrumental in retention of the basic values propogated by the state without much dilution through external sources. Religion has been used positively and continues to have a strong influence in the lives of the people. Helping the community through social work, giving of alms, charity, etc. are encouraged and rewarded socially. This is also responsible for the high level of motivation among cadres doing work for community welfare.

Finally, there is the question of the role of women in community development. It is being increasingly recognised that the women have an important role to play in not just the welfare of the family but the community and society at large. In India the women have lagged behind their counterparts in Indonesia in terms of health, nutrition, education and the general level of awareness and social mobilisation. The literacy rate for the females in India was 39 per cent according to the 1991 Census compared to 64 per cent for males. Similarly, the work participation rate in 1991 was only 25 per cent for women against 52 per cent for men. In Indonesia the literacy for women was 78 per cent for women against 89 per cent of men in 1990. The work participation rates are also more impressive, specially in skilled and technical employment. The higher level of education among women is responsible for lower infant mortality rate and lower total fertility rate in Indonesia compared to India. The role of women in community development in Indonesia is nowhere more evident than in formation of cadres at village level, the institution of "Dharma Wanita" consisting of wives of Government servants, and the lead role played by them in the family welfare movement.

However, one should not lose sight of the fact that India is a vast country with population close to 950 million compared to 190 million people living in Indonesia. The magnitude and the complexity of the problems of community development in India present a much greater challenge than anywhere else. Despite the constraints mentioned above, commendable work has been done in several parts of the country in the area of rural and community development. The catalysts for change have sometimes been Government officials, sometimes NGOs and sometimes dynamic leaders and grassroot workers. The importance of human resource development and the significant role of women in transforming community life are now fully realised and committed to by the Indian Government. The recent amendment to the Indian Constitution and the enactment of the Panchayati Raj Act for establishment of local self government possesses great potential and promise for bringing about a sea change in community participation and development in the years to come.

10

DEVELOPMENTAL PLAs

— ANIL C. SHAH

Participatory Learning and Action (PLA) can be put to many uses : for appraising a situation—facts and perception; for planning; for monitoring and evaluation etc. As a development practitioner I have been concerned with negotiating terms of collaboration with village communities, to work out the meeting ground between local community's agenda and our (development agency)'s agenda. Earlier development programmes claiming allegiance to participatory approach usually had a firm agenda and fixed targets. The development agencies wanted the 'beneficiaries' to participate in their programme by appreciating and abiding by agency's terms or they would lose the benefit! When such one sided agenda approach failed, development agencies have been trying to develop approaches which recognize that every community, indeed every family has its own agenda and therefore development agencies may better try to evolve a fit between agency's agenda and local agenda. I have been employing PLA approach and techniques since 1987 to learn about local community's perceptions—knowledge about the issues, its importance, priority, stakes etc., and to find a meeting ground to negotiate the terms of collaboration. This is possible only if the development agency has flexibility, not in its basic principles which may be non-negotiable, but in its systems and procedures, and it should not be under the pressure of time bound targets.

Two experiences will illustrate and substantiate applicability of PLA approach in furthering development programmes committed to participatory approach.

Check Dams for Groundwater Recharge

In 1993, as the team leader of Aga Khan Rural Support Programme India, AKRSP(I), I faced a problem about farmers' readiness to participate and contribute to organisation's check dam scheme. Water tables in the wells were going down for which a solution demanded by the farmers and acceptable to the organisation was rain water harvesting structures like checkdams that would recharge the wells.

Apart from the vitiated environment by government constructing such structures free, there was a real problem of uncertainty where the underground currents go, which of them benefit farmers and how much. The field staff complained that they spend too much time in persuading farmers to make contribution.

We set out to conduct a PLA in village Chandwana to develop a method of dialoguing and negotiating that would bring both the parties closer. Though we did not plan in advance detailed techniques for PLA, we were clear about the intended outcome:

(1) Importance of well irrigation in the economy of the village, the magnitude of the problem of falling ground water levels, its impact on agriculture;
(2) Farmers perception about the relationship between check dams and water tables; and
(3) Their assessment about the performance of the check dams constructed so far and how quality of new structures could be improved.

Water Resources Map

The first exercise was to get an overview of the water resources of the village. The villagers were able to quickly draw a map indicating the flows of water in the village and the location of wells as well as existing check dams on the streams. The second exercise was to bring out the knowledge of the farmers about the history of development of wells in the village.

Chart - I indicates data over a period of 40 years—number of wells, the depth when water was found, the cost of sinking a well and the certainty of striking water. This chart clearly brought out that with rapid increase in the number of wells from mere 7 in 1950 to 400 in 1990, the water level has fallen from 30 feet to more than 150 feet, the cost which was about Rs. 3000 in 1950 has risen to about Rs. 1,30,000.

Ground Water Scenario — A Time Series

Chart - 10.1

Time Series on Growth of Irrigation Wells Village Chandwana

Junagadh District, Gujarat, India

Year	1950	1960	1970	1980	1990
No of wells	7	100	150	200	400
Depth of well when water will be available	30'	30'	45'	100'	150'
Expenditure per well (including (Rupees) submersible pump)	3000	5000	1000	12000	1,30,000
Certainty of striking water	100%	100%	100%	80%	50%

On the other hand the certainty of striking water which was almost 100 per cent till 1970 has come down to 50 per cent. That means even after spending Rs. 1,30,000 the certainity of getting water was only 50 per cent, and there may be equal chance of the whole investment turning out wasteful.

The discussion about the meaning of what was revealed by this information led to the need for recharging the ground water through construction of check dams. However, there were already 4 check dams constructed by government agencies and only one of them was serving the purpose of storing water contributing to groundwater recharge. The remaining 3 were poor in quality and therefore water flowed through the foundation and even through the wall of the check dam. The farmers wanted reconstruction of these check dams which were on good sites. When the question of quality of new check dams came, the farmers had natural reaction of passing on the responsibility to AKRSP which had already constructed several check dams of good quality and therefore, they expressed confidence that if AKRSP constructs check dams in the village, they would be of good quality. We, therefore, explained to them that after all even a Voluntary Organisation like AKRSP was getting its staff who were brought up in the same families and who were trained in the same institutions as the staff of government agencies. They could also indulge into malpractice of misappropriating cement and compromising on quality which will lead to construction of weak structures. What would AKRSP staff lose if the new structures were equally bad? They might be punished, transferred or even sacked, but to our question "who will be the real sufferers", all the farmers gave the obvious reply: the farmers of the village. They agreed that they had the real long term stake in ensuring quality in the construction of check dams. That took us to the next exercise.

What makes for good quality in construction: The farmers discussed and noted on a chart paper the following essential features of a good quality check dam:

1. There needs to be storing of water without seepage.
2. Sturdy construction is needed which should last at least 25 years.
3. There should be arrangement of desilting and repairs.
4. Direct pumping of stored water should be prohibited.

The last phase of discussion after these exercises were conducted, reached the common ground where the agency and the farmers' group agreed that even though AKRSP had technical staff, unless the farmers were involved in ensuring quality during construction, the structures may not be as good as the farmers desired. It was then agreed that the farmers could select from among themselves members who will constitute a construction committee. AKRSP would train them into technical aspects which will help them to ensure quality during construction. The farmers also agreed that they will raise funds to make contribution to convince AKRSP of their commitment to join hands with AKRSP and also to collect fund which will be available to the farmers organisation for meeting the repairs requirements after the check dam was completed. AKRSP is following this PLA exercise which has helped it to conduct dialogues and arrive at negotiated agreement about farmers' participation and contribution for construction of check dams. The number of check dams constructed has increased over the years from 7 in 1993 when this exercise was developed, to 13 in 1994, 16 in 1995, 40 in 1996. According to the feedback received, the success rate of PLA outcome is 90 per cent. We would have been happy even with success rate of 60 per cent. More satisfactory development is that there is hardly any need for such PLA exercises. Village communities approach AKRSP with proposals for checkdams with readiness to participate in terms of responsibility and contribution.

Our second experience is more recent, relating to August 1996.

Farmer Managed Canal

Our present organisation, Development Support Centre, has promoted a farmers' organisation to take over the management of a distributory of a government canal forming part of the command area of a major irrigation project of Dharoi in North Gujarat, India. The society is registered and the rehabilitation of the existing structures is completed. Very soon the farmers' irrigation cooperative would take over the management from the government irrigation department. We wanted to find out as to what extent the farmers were clear about what is involved in taking over the management of a government canal. We knew that there were 5 tube wells in the same village which were set up by groups of farmers. These tube wells requiring investment of about Rs. 300,000 each, are known as "company tube wells" even though there is no formal organisation with any legal entity. However, there are large number of such tube wells which are functioning very satisfactorily in this area. Our agenda for a meeting with the leaders of the irrigation cooperative in August 1996, was to find out: (a) farmers' perception of the role of water in agriculture production, and (b) to what extent the irrigation society would be willing to apply the principles and working procedures of company tube wells management, to the management of the canal when 'turned over' to them.

The first exercise was to list our items that were crucial for good agricultural production. They listed out the following 13 points:

1. Fertility of land
2. Deep tillage
3. Quality seeds
4. Farmyard manure
5. Fertilizer
6. Plant protection
7. Inter-cultivation

8. Timely irrigation
9. Protection of crops
10. Financial resources
11. Market price
12. Availability of labour
13. Crop rotation.

We then asked them to indicate their priorities through allotting marks out of 100 for which we used grain seeds, the importance of each of the eight factors in "Kharif season" during monsoon period when if there are normal rains there may not arise need for providing support irrigation. Some old farmers insisted that only three factors were crucial as was said in the old proverb, "It is the tillage, manure and water that bring prosperity to farmers." However, other farmers knew that other factors were also important and gave their scoring as shown below:

Chart 10.2

Factors Determining Agriculture Production

Factors No.		Comparative Percentage of marks Kharif	Rabi
1.	Fertility of land	17	13
2.	Deep tillage	17	12
3.	Quality seeds	17	13
4.	Farmyard manure	5	
5.	Fertilizer	5	10
6.	Plant protection	2	5
7.	Inter cultivation	5	
8.	Timely irrigation	5	22
9.	Protection of crops	10	5
10.	Financial resources	2	5
11.	Market price	5	3
12.	Availability of labour	5	10
13.	Crop rotation	5	2
	Total Marks	100	100

For 'rabi' season, when the crops are raised only through irrigation, they allocated 22 marks to irrigation and the rest 78 were distributed as shown in chart 10.2 above.

After appreciating the primacy importance of irrigation in agricultural production in winter and summer seasons, the next exercise was about what constituted good irrigation system. The farmers group presented their considered views on a chart paper as under:

1. Planning for rabi irrigation,
2. Adequate water distribution,
3. Availability of water when required for crop growth,
4. Maintenance of distributory/sub-minor,
5. Distribution to farmers according to turn,
6. Recovery of water charges according to water use,
7. Satisfaction to tail enders, and
8. Good irrigation reflected in agriculture production.

The group was then asked to give comparative scoring to each of these factors out of 10 marks for the canal as managed by the government. Using again grain seeds they allotted marks out of 10 for each item. They were then asked to give marks for the same factors in 'company' tube wells. There are also wells in the village from which the owners sell water to neighbouring farmers. Some farmers owned their own source of water, surface wells or tube wells. The group could quickly assign marks out of 10 to each of the factors for the remaining three categories of water source—the 'company' tube wells, the private tube wells selling water to others and farmers' own wells. Chart 10.3 was prepared within 15 minutes.

The farmers then were asked to prepare one more chart which indicated difference of marks for all the factors between government managed system and company tube wells. Chart 10.4 below brings out very vividly the perception of the farmers that for important factors, the government system scores poorly as compared to the remaining three systems. The difference being as large as 9 points in the distribution of water and 8 to 5 points in terms of other criteria. Only in one factor namely collection of water charges, the government agency had impressed the farmers by its competence.

With these charts before them the common ground was reached for discussing the issue about the future management of canal when it would be 'turned over' to them. The farmers in village Thalota had already the experience of managing irrigation sources which appeared to be working far more satisfactorily than the government managed

Chart 10.3

	Factors	Comparative Scoring (Maximum Marks is 10 for each Factor)			
		Present Management of Canal	Company Tube Well	Private Tube Well	Owners' Well
1.	Planning for Rabi irrigation	5	8	10	10
2.	Adequate water distribution	3	8	8	8
3.	Availability of water when required for crop growth	5	10	10	10
4.	Maintenance of distributory/ sub-minor	1	7	7	7
5.	Distribution to farmers according to turn	1	10	10	10
6.	Recovery of water charges according to water use	10	9	9	10
7.	Satisfaction to tail enders	2	10	10	—
8.	Good irrigation reflected in agriculture production	7	9	9	10

canal. When they would take over the government canal, will they be able to manage it as satisfactorily on all counts as the company tube wells? How would this be done? The author suggested that the members of the irrigation society may work out later the detailed steps and the arrangement required to run the government canal very close to the principles and systems they had evolved in managing company tube wells. The author have been repeatedly mentioning that government canal, when 'turned over' for management to the farmers' organisation should be considered as one more 'company tubewell'. We left the issue to be discussed by them later, considering in detail each factor that determined good water management.

There was almost an agreement on one important item of our agenda—the water rate that the society would charge to its members. The calculations brought out that in case of company tube wells the water rate was charged on hourly basis and same was true for private tube wells selling water. It came to almost Rs. 2000 per acre for wheat crop. Though the farmers thought it to be outrageous that such rate could be applied for supplying water from government canals, when

Chart 10.4

Towards More Satisfactory Management of Irrigation Canals
Maximum Marks

	Factors	Comparative Scoring (Maximum is 10 for each factor)		
		Present Manag-ement of Canal	Company Tube well	Distance in marks scored
1.	Distribution to farmers according to turn	1	10	9
2.	Maintenance of distributory sub-minor	1	7	6
3.	Satisfaction to tail enders	2	10	8
4.	Availability of water when required for crop growth	5	10	5
5.	Adequate water distribution	3	8	5
6.	Planning for rabi irrigation	5	8	3
7.	Agriculture production	7	9	2
8.	Recovery of water charges according to water use	10	10	0

the government agency was charging only Rs. 50 per acre, they were willing to consider the issue in terms of percentage of what was being charged in case of company tube wells. Though firm decision was not taken it appeared certain that the water rate may be fixed at Rs. 100 per acre for raising wheat crop. Though double than government rate, it may be only 5 per cent of what was being charged from the company/ private tube wells.

From Top Down Approach to Developmental PLA

What has these exercises achieved? Certainly not the empowerment in terms of villagers, and special interest groups anlaysing and deciding without any constraints, their situation, problems, opportunities and priorities. Only a few programmes are so flexible and open to accommodate in unrestricted manner, the local priorities and extend financial and other supports. Most of the development agencies may not even be equipped to handle such diverse portfolio. Most of the rural development programmes have some focus, basic parameters in terms of principles, almost preconditions, for extending support. The challenge before a development agency is to work out with village groups the terms of collaboration that will make the agency's programme acceptable to villagers with a sense of ownership. This would require that the village community is helped, step by step through a sequence using their own experience, in reaching a vision of development which has inspired the programme and motivated the development agency. As David Mosse points out in his extremely valuable paper. "People's Knowledge In Project Planning" even "participatory planning often conspires to produce consensus, concealing underlying differences of interest and motivation." If such PLA approach is conducted mechanically without sensitivity to local variations, there is a possibility that "it may not be grounded socially in a coherent set of social ties and common interest, and PLA may revert to RRA." But what is suggested here is a process of bringing to surface people's knowledge of local situation and helping people to appreciate the movement from their short-term, individual-centred perspective to long-term community based goals and action. In the process it may develop, as David Mosse would like, "villagers own awareness, skills and confidence in problem analysis, and planning." Even though not as open minded as one would like, such PLA would take an agency a long way from the usual agency planned targets in which people are coaxed or lured to participate with very unsatisfactory results in terms of post project care, management and impact.

Literature on PRA—PRL emphasizes the exercises to help in discovering the hidden capacities of villages to map, diagrams score and rank that enhance the quality of the information. Robert Chambers does refer to PRA—PLA "creating that relaxed rapport which is crucial to facilitating participation." A development practitioner is indeed interested in discovering villagers' talents and in creation of relaxed rapport but for a development worker 'participation' is not an abstract concept. When PLA helps in negotiating a match between the community agenda and its own, a development agency takes to PLA approach and techniques for furtherance of a programme in more satisfactory manner. PLA helps the agency in overcoming the barrier of established local leadership which would like to corner the benefits and in mitigating the brunt of the arrogance of agency's management and professionals and brings about a negotiated fit that enhances the successful outcome of a development scheme. This is development PLA, which is based on the premises : (a) development agency has developed a programme, usually after studies and experiments, which it considers to be good for an area or certain groups, (b) that the local community would be largely in agreement with the goals of the programme, (c) there is need to help the local community/groups to analyse their problems and past experiences and work out the implications of various options for solution, and (d) reach an agreement with the development agency about the adoption of the programme and modalities of collaboration. This may not be full empowerment, but much better than the usual top down approach which requires the local community/groups to 'take it or leave it.' Developmental PLA is hopefully a long stride from the topdown approach.

THE MORAL FABRIC OF COMMUNITY PARTICIPATION
Ethics and Values

11

PROCESS OF CONFLICT RESOLUTION IN PARTICIPATORY FOREST MANAGEMENT

A Case Study from Sarugarh Range, North Bengal, India

S.B. ROY, GANESH YADAV AND RAKTIMA MUKHERJEE

Conflict and cooperation characterize societies of any social animals particularly of human beings. In its extreme animalistic form conflict calls for complete annihilation or elimination of the opposition. On the other hand, cooperation may take the form of unquestioning obedience and servitude. The extreme animalistic forms are evident in the primitive and authoritarian societies.

To ensure dynamism and for sustaining progress human societies need democracy and popular participation that is neither violent nor servile. Only men are capable of conflict resolution in this non-animalistic way to the point of equilibrium. Then, of course, newer issues of conflict will arise to be resolved in the same way. Democracy and development will thus move on in tandem.

When individuals or group competing for a scarce resource not only try to block others from reaching it but also attempt to neutralize, injure, or eliminate their rivals, conflict occurs (Coser, 1956). Where conflict is intense, these attempts to block others may result in overt hostility, injury, defeat or even annihilation. Conflict between the superpowers, for example, carries the threat of nuclear disaster and the potential destruction of society.

A certain amount of conflict is always present in society. It may even have positive consequences. When a group experiences conflict with outsiders, group members often draw closer together and achieve a greater sense of solidarity (Coser, 1956; Simmel, 1955). For example, although Britain's dispute with Argentina over the Falkland Islands cost billions of dollars and hundreds of lives, it also became a rallying point of the Thatcher administration in its effort to demonstrate Britain's strength and military superiority and to restore the pride of the nation.

When conflict takes place within groups, however, the effect is seldom positive. The result is usually destruction of the group or significant alteration in its members' relationships. Win, lose, or draw, conflict changes the relationship. Within groups, it is a process of change, not stability.

In the context of India's endeavour to ensure democracy at the grassroots as well as her efforts to eliminate the potentially explosive rural poverty, the attempts to conflict resolution in the poorest of the poor forest communities and participatory forest management have become enormously significant. A case study from West Bengal amply exemplifies it.

To go into the details of applied principles of conflict resolution, let us look at the following aspects of conflict and its management :

(1) What is conflict?
(2) How it emerges?
(3) What causes conflict?
(4) Different faces of conflict?
(5) Methods of conflict management,
(6) How the methods are used : A case study?
(7) Post-script of conflict management.

Conflict is an open and direct struggle of individuals or groups against others. It is essentially emotional and violent and opposed to any attempts to cool reasoning and agreement, mutual cooperation and accommodation.

Conflict emerges out a perceived threat to the self-interest of the individual or the group. So it has external as well as internal manifestations. Internally, feelings of deprivation, injustice and loss can either be pronounced or remain somewhat vague and uncertain. Externally power over all kinds of possessions, be they material and intellectual property or mates, acquisition of status, freedom of action and thought or any other desired values are clearly discernible at various levels. They range from softer competition, arguments, non-cooperation even indifference, litigation, struggles for establishing philosophical and scientific ideas and sometimes disturbing the opponents' means to achieve their goals to ruthless conflicts in religious or race wars, class-wars, individual or group terrorism etc.

Behind any conflict there is a lack of communication and misinformation, misinterpretation and misuse of correct information and illogical value systems. No wonder conflicts have been a natural process in human society. So is the conflict resolution management.

The Joint Forest Management (JFM) programme of West Bengal and other parts India has opened avenues to researchers from social sciences and management domain to learn the process of change and factors responsible for the new programme (Roy, 1993).

Villagers may differ from the angles of caste, class, occupation, age, sex etc., but they need a common goal for resource management. Experience in community forestry programme has shown that conflict is essentially based on inequity and inequality. They can be classified as follows :

Classification of Conflict Based on Inequity and Inequality

Inequity is very much present in respect of gender and its access to and control of resources.

Inequality manifests in :

(1) Gender,
(2) Religion,
(3) Nationality,
(4) Race,
(5) Political ethos,
(6) Occupation, and
(7) Distribution of resources.

Stakeholders have different interests and goals. Each of the stakeholders tries to achieve goal by different means and actions. This happens because of weak institutional norms, rules and regulations and lack of trust among the partners. After a lengthy period dominated by economic considerations and growth, the human factor has resumed its rightful place, both as the driving force and the ultimate recipient of development (Huynth Cao tr, *et al.* 1986). Human beings develop their own identity based on socialisation, further through education and employment. Here lies the importance of sensitization. It is one of the vital processes to educate people to make them aware of reality and motivate them to resolve disputed issues.

What is Sensitization ? Its Redeeming Features

Sensitization enables people to come out of their shell of prejudices and narrowly perceived world. After sensitization a person can test the reality with reasonings and from an objective view-point, using his/her experience, seeking alternative solutions and estimating the consequences of each alternative step (Roy, 1992). Reality testing will be in the form of separating facts from fantasy, opinions, feelings and even traditions, Sensitization includes perceiving and evaluating the prevailing situation and relating the factual date to past knowledge and experience. After sensitization one can take calculated risk, not just jump into action out of enthusiasm and impulses. Even the risk taking is base on realistic, dependable and complete information strengthening a person's ability to gather, organize and evaluate information more accurately. His/her own learning, experience and awareness can be evaluated by himself. Sometimes his/her inner conflicts or interactions between his/her own ego states are consciously evaluated (at the psychic level) and past assumptions are accepted or rejected on the basis of reality needs and appropriateness. Thus a sensitized person is mentally prepared for conflict resolution. His/Her mental state becomes really fire-proof even though at times it may appear to be defensive. She/he becomes an unbiased spectator, capable of resolving problems and conflicts calmly and happily.

Approaches to Manage Conflict

There are some basic steps towards conflict management. They are:

(1) Self sensitization—understanding one's own self and interactions of ego states;
(2) Active listening;
(3) Maintaining eye contact with the people spoken to;
(4) Recognizing the strength of the people and praising them sincerely;
(5) Respecting common ground and identity;
(6) Giving correct information, if information is inadequate, using non-verbal communication such as gesture or tone;
(7) Seeking options and suggestions;
(8) Respecting values;
(9) Pragmatic planning emanating from the people;
(10) Having precise commitments—what, how, when, who, where;

and

(11) Monitoring plans of action.

The above approaches would be meaningful in the context of a case study.

It was at Sarugarh, North Bengal. The forest was fast depleting. With considerable efforts specially on the part of the Range officer, a forest protection committee (FPC) was formed. For a systematic and well-monitored collection of fuel by the community members, identity cards were issued.

The community members were refugees from the neighbouring country and even the women were quite vocal about their demands. The proximity of the large town centre, Siliguri, created additional pressure on the use and sale of the forest products. The forest was deteriorating rapidly and the forest department was worried and seemed to be helpless. There was tense conflict situation between the FD and the Forest Community (FC).

At this stage IBRAD came into picture to help resolve the conflict and come out with a micro plan for the development of the forest community.

IBRAD researchers and faculty members met quite a few people of the community in front of a temple. They all sat on the ground and disclosed their identity—that they were from an NGO in Calcutta, they all had heard about their FPC, one of the earliest FPCs in West Bengal. The IBRAD people wanted to know the methods of running the FPC, to learn from them as students.

The villagers were, however, very vocal and came out with the following charter of demands :

(1) Provision of fuel for all.
(2) Valid identity cards to be issued and respected by the forest department officials so that fuel collection was not hindered.
(3) The local forest ranger must to be removed.
(4) The FD must come to terms with the villagers.

Seeing the tense feeling of the villages, IBRAD people tried to diffuse the emotional outbursts and started an exercise on resource mapping. They spread a big piece of chart paper on the ground and requested the villagers to teach them about the village, its resources, forest etc. and draw a map of the village. After some hesitation one villager came forward and began to draw the map. Slowly curiosity was aroused and those who were around contributed either to map preparation and discussion or just discussion throughout the map making (conflict resolution) process.

The objective was not to develop a good and correct map of the village, but to get men and women involved in some activities. The IBRAD people have learnt from their past experience that however much the villagers remain critical about the development programmes imposed from outside, a different kind of relationship is built up when they work together. Moreover, when people share information about their own village, its roads, wells, paddy fields, ponds, trees, schools, temples etc. they shift from critical positions to cold facts. When the field worker submits himself or herself as a learner with all humility, villagers then feel proud of their knowledge, feel important and are willing to share their indigenous knowledge with the outsider. These activities help develop work relationship between the villagers and the outsiders and among the villagers themselves. Women also come forward and sometimes indicate the mistakes made by others during the mapping exercise. They substantially contribute to the mapping process.

More than 100 men, women and children assembled around the 'outsiders'. It was evident that the critical behaviour against the foresters was reduced because the foresters present there were also asking questions to the villagers about the mapping. They had also sat down on the ground, at the same level with others.

Now the foresters had to collect information on the demography profile and the actual needs of the villagers. The foresters were asking questions and the villagers' answers were being noted by foresters on the printed format of the Forest Department. It was also seen by the researchers of IBRAD that the expectation of the villagers were raised higher and higher when questions like 'how many of you can be employee?', 'Do you need fuel?', 'What kind of employment do you require?', Do you need drinking water form the government well?', 'Do you need roads to be constructed by the government?' were asked.

Being tuned to the nation of a popular government dishing out everything they need, the villagers perceived that whenever any government official asked such questions, he was certainly going to give something to the villagers. So they often shifted from fact finding attitude to the begging one and demanded a lot of things which was not possible for any government to provide. Here the villagers demanded:

(1) Employment for all,

(2) Fuel for all,
(3) Construction of a lozenge factory,
(4) Establishment of sewing centres,
(5) Construction of good roads
(6) Provision of drinking water facilities
(7) Initiating special schemes for employment.

All these were faithfully recorded by the foresters.

The researchers and the first author as facilitator, were all listening to the problems and expectations of the villagers. The first author quietly intercepted and posed some questions to them : Is it possible for the government to provide employment for all? Can the central or state government do it? The forest department is only a tiny part of a government. The range officer's is again a negligible post of the department. How can the officer meet all your demands? If you ask for more than what the department can offer you, are you not heading for the impossible?

Surprisingly they all admitted the demands were too high and unrealistic. They admitted that the forest was the only sustaining factor for their living and they must protect and enlarge it for their own survival. Their grievances against the range officer and the department boiled down to only two things : (i) the villagers must be treated like human beings, (ii) the identity cards issued by the department must be respected by all its officers. They must not contradict themselves. The villagers assured the facilitators of proper care of the forest if a meaningful joint management is ensured.

When the researchers and facilitators were about to get up, the villagers specially invited them : "Please come again to our village. We have enjoyed your company and talks very much. We have never seen any official sitting on the floor."

The first author as said, "We are very happy to meet you and spend some time with you. I am sure that there will be good cooperation between you and the forest department. I will come again to see a good forest".

One of the villagers who looked like a leader said, "Yes, we are also happy to hear good words from you. Please suggest how best we can go about the FPC"?

Suddenly an idea flashed in and the first author thought, "If the people have so much good will and love for us because we listened to them for a while, why not try this *power of love* in resolving the conflict with range officer? After all, he has done a lot for the villagers, moved from door to door to form the FPC, sincerely devoted his energy to protect and enlarge the forest!" So he said, "The power is with you and you can do it".

The villagers looked on eagerly. The first author said, "Can you do one thing for my sake?" They answered they could with pleasure. The first author assured them that they could change the range officer instantly. "How is that possible?"—One surprised villager burst out. The first author smiled and said, "Will you do what I say?" The villagers answered in one voice, "yes, of course". Then the first author came out with his idea. "Just tell the Range officer," You are a good range officer. You have come to our village. We are grateful to you. We want to protect the forest. We want to have your help and we will support you."

All the villagers were quiet. No one responded. It was evidently very difficult for them to say good words for the range officer. Then the facilitator said, "What happened? You the simple innocent villagers are rich in one thing - the *power of love*. Show it to the range officer and this will surely change his heart. Can't you do this for me? Even if it looks artificial or mechanical, please do it and see for yourself what happens. The rest I will take care of.

The villagers agreed to do for the facilitator who advised them to go to the nearby training centre for forest officials at about 10 a.m. and say what he had asked them to say in presence of the District Forest Officer (DFO) with due respect to the range officer.

The villagers promised to do so and said, "We will also show him that we are not bad people and we all want the forest department to work for us."

Next morning in the midst of the training programme, the villagers came in a large group in the form of a procession. They brought garlands. They entered the camp where many forest officials including the Chief Conservator of Forests (CCF), DFO and range officers were present. The villagers put the garland round the neck of the range officer and said, "Sir, we have come for you and need your help. You have come to our village for our benefit. We are grateful to you."

The range officer could not anticipate it. He was visibly shocked and overwhelmed with emotion. He lowered his head down to receive the garland. He then said in a choked voice : "I never knew so many villagers are with me. I never knew so many villagers love me. I promise I will go to the village. I will go there next Tuesday and will try to start some schemes for you."

What lesson do we derive from this real life case study? Let us list them here:

(1) The whole story may appear very simplistic. But if we delve into the matter a little deeper, we will realize that the simple tool that emerged out of experience and research of different disciplines is essentially love, empathy and objective concern for the resolution of conflicts.
(2) The tools will be effective when we clearly understand the logic of our approaches.
(3) For emotion-free management of conflict, self-sensitization is of utmost importance.
(4) To spread the gospel of conflict management, short workshops and manuals are helpful.
(5) In the same way follow-up and process documentation of conflict management at different places can go a long way to help management workers.
(6) Conflict management is done in various ways all over the world. Many of them are well-documented. Collection of bibliography and sharing through networking are vital for our efforts.

Acknowledgements

Authors express their sincere gratitude to Mr. S. Roy, IFS, (then CF), the Divisional Forest Officer, the Range officer of Sarugarh Range and other forest officials for extending all possible support and participating in the process. Villagers deserve appreciation for providing us an opportunity for learning while working with them. Without them this experiment of "How to resolve conflict" would not have been successful. Our sincere thanks go to Debabrata Ghosh, educationist for editing the research paper. We are thankful to Indranil Bhattacharya for computerising the paper.

REFERENCES

Bendix, Reinhard. "Bureaucracy and the Problem of Power," In Merton, *et al.* (eds.) *Reader in Bureaucracy.* (Glencoe: Free Press, 1952, 114-134.)

Collins, Randall. *Conflict Sociology* (New York : Academic Press, 1975).

Coser, Lewis A. (1955). *The Functions of Social Conflict.* Glencoe, III. Free Press.

Dahrendorf, Ralf. (1971). *Class and Class Conflict in Industrial Society.* Standford, Calif,: Standford University Press.

Dhyani, S.K. (1980). *Chipko Andolan, Kyon our Kaise?* (In Hindi), Himalaya, 4(6): 29-32.

Freeman, David M. (1974). *Technology and Society : Issues in Assessment, Conflict, and Choice.* Chicago: Rand - MacNally.

Gecas, Victor. (1981). "Contexts of socialization." In morris Rosenberg & Ralph H. Turner (Eds.), *Social Psychology : Sociological Perspectives* (pp.165-199). New York : Basic Books.

Malhotra, K.C., D.Deb, T.S. Vasulu, M. Dutta, G. Yadav and M. Adhikari. (1991), *Role of non-Timber Forest Produce in Village Economy : A Household Survey in Jamboni Range Midnapore District,* West Bengal, IBRAD, Calcutta.

Malhotra, K.C. and M., Poffenberger, (1989). (Ed.) *Forest Protection through Community Participation.* Working paper, West Bengal Forest Department, West Bengal, India.

Marx, Gary T. (Ed.). (1971). *Racial Conflict.* Boston : Little, Brown.

Murdock, G.P. (1949). *Social Structure,* N.Y.: Macmillan, pp.387.

Oberschall, A. (1973). *Social Conflict and Social Movements,* Englewood Cliffs, N.J.: Prentice-Hall.

"Participatory Rural Appraisal Handbook" Resources Management Support Series No. 1. The National Environ. Secretariat, Govt. of Kenya Clark University, Egerton Univ. The Centre for International Development and Environment of the World Resource Institute.

Parajuli, Pramod. (1991). "Power and Knowledge in Development Discourse: New Social Movements and the State in India". *International Social Science Journal:* International Conflict Research, No. 127 : 173-190.

Phillip, Viegas and Geeta Menon (1991). Forest Protection Committees of West Bengal : Role and Participation of Women. Paper prepared for the ILO workshop on "Women and Wasteland Development", New Delhi.

Ritzer, George. (1977). *Working : Conflict and Change* (2nd ed.). Englewood Cliffs, N.J.: Prentice-Hall.

Roy, S.B. (1991). Forest Protection Committees in West Bengal, India : Emerging Policy Issues. Working paper prepared on Social Forestry, Environment Policy Institute, East West Centre, Hawaii.

Roy, S.B. and Mitali, Chatterjee (1990). *Manual for Orientation Course on the Microplanning Through Participatory Forest Management System.* Working paper of IBRAD, Calcutta.

Singh, A.K. *et al.* (1987). *Forest Resource, Economy and Environment.* New Delhi : Concept Publishing Co.

Smelser, Neil J. (1962). *Theory of Collective Behaviour.* New York : Free Press.

Star, Akos. (1984). *Culture and Power.* Sage Publishing.

Stryker, Sheldon. (1981). "Symbolic interactionism : Themes and variations." In Morris Rosenberg & Ralph H. Turner (Eds.), *Social Psychology : Sociological Perspectives* (pp. 3-29). New York : Basic Books.

Suttles, G.D. (1972). *The Social Construction of Communities.* Chicago, University of Chicago Press.

Toennies, Ferdinand. *Community and Society (1887),* trans. & Ed. Charles A. Lommis. (East Lansing : Michigan State University Press, 1957)

Turner, Ralph H. (1964). "Collective Behaviour." In R.E.L. Faris (Ed.), *Handbook of Modern Sociology* (pp.382-425). Chicago: Rand- McNally.

Weber, Max. (1970a). "Bureaucracy." In H.H. Gerth & C. Wright Mills (Trans.), *From Max Weber: Essays in Sociology* (pp.196-240). New York: Oxford University Press. (Original work published 1910).

Wellman, Barry. (1979). " The Community Question: The Intimate networks of East Yorkers." *American Journal of Sociology,* 84(March): 1201-1231.

Zurcher, Louis A. (1977). *The Mutable Self: A Self-Concept for Change.* Beverly Hills, Calif.: Sage Publications.

12

POVERTY ALLEVIATION AND THE PRA OF ETHICS

— INDIRA KOHLI

The girl painfully lifted herself up from the floor and slowly pulled her *kameez* over her hump. "Who is going to look at you? everyone turns away, frightened of the bad luck you bring. Look at us, we have to look at you and what is our condition?" The man shouted as she shuffled towards the drum in which the ingredients were fermenting. She had forgotten how to cry, to laugh, to play. She only knew that she had to make the alcohol on the sale of which she and her parents survived.

She had not been born with a hunched back, but she had forgotten she had ever stood upright. Her only memory of her early years was the excruciating pain she experienced as she lay twisted on the rocks below the cliff. She vaguely remembered running to prevent the calf from straying too near the edge of the mountain but her sudden dash had caused the animal to leap away. The earth crumbled beneath its feet and as it fell the girl also tumbled down the cliff-side.

Through the long winter months she had lain on a rug on the floor along the side wall of the hut. No one washed or cleaned her. Summer came and her mother dragged her outside on the rug into the tiny courtyard, where again she lay. Once, just once she asked to be cleaned but her father's reply was "Who killed our female calf? the only means of our future livelihood?".

One night she heard her parents discussing her future and she knew she had to get up and help her mother in the alcoholic liquor trade or she would be swept away in the monsoon stream with her parents sounding an alarm only when there would no longer be hope of her survival. She pulled herself to her knees and then with infinitesimally slow movement she pulled herself to her feet. She swayed with weakness. She could not stand upright because her back was now permanently damaged. "Let me help you mother" she whispered as she shuffled towards her. "Here, pick up the ladle and stir, and keep stirring until I tell you to stop" was the reply. Her mother's position as wife in the household was perilous for she had produced only one female child and she lived in terror of the day when her husband would tell her to go home to visit her parents, for she knew he would immediately remarry and she would never be able to return. And the girl? Take her home to her parents as her only achievement?

Mother, please teach me how to make the alcohol then you can help father and I will do this work" whispered the girl. The woman stood still, looking at her daughter, the deformed back, crookedly splayed fingers and head permanently bent to one side. If she felt a spasm of compassion, she hid it. "Come" she ordered and the lesson began. The girl was soon adept at the job of brewing alcohol and within a year she was making the best country liquor in the *gram sabha.*

She never had time to play, but then, she did not know how to play. The girls of her age avoided her because their parents frightened them with the consequences of the evil eye of hunch-backed people.

Her village nestled on the terrace of a hill slope. The neighbouring mountains were bare of trees for they had been lopped over the years. Now not even stumps remained. Her mother had to daily trudge far uphill to collect firewood from the remaining forested areas.

One day, a young girl shouted in excitement "Strangers are coming, strangers are coming"! The women immediately disappeared into their homes or busied themsleves with chores of feeding animals, sweeping, cooking. No one reprimanded the young girl who continued to report the progress of the strangers. "Oh, she's sat down on a rock, she's old" she reported, her voice heavy with disappointment. "She's up, she's walking faster. The two men are walking behind her". Two men and a woman. "What do they want here, we have nothing to give them" said the aunt of the hunchback. "Let's see" said a friend, "They may be selling something". "They may be coming to ask questions", "Oh no, let us go to collect wood from the forest otherwise they will catch hold of us and we'll be stuck all afternoon" and the women picked up their scythes and ran up the hill at the back of the village.

The young girl had just finished pouring the alcohol into bottles and she sat down for a well-earned rest. "Ten bottles of liquor" she calculated "I'll carry them up tonight. I think father will be pleased".

Suddenly, someone knocked on the door. The young girl thinking it may be a customer, opened it and to her amazement she found an old woman standing in front of her. The young girl was non-plussed. "Does she want a bottle?" She wondered, but instinctively knew the woman had not come to buy or sell anything. The woman smiled and the young girl was overcome with shyness. She hid behind the door but secretly prayed that the woman would stay. "Come let me look at you", called the woman gently but the young girl was now in a panic. The old woman put her head around the door, and catching the young girl, a spring doe, by the hand she inched her out from behind it. "How did this happen?", she asked, stroking the hump. As far back as the young girl could remember it was the first time anyone had even touched her hump. The children had poked it with sticks, mimicked her, laughed at her, spat as she passed them, but no, no one had touched the hump. "How did it happen, you fell didn't you" the old woman asked as she stroked the girl who turned, fled into the hut and slammed the door.

The young girl hooked up the chain latch and peeped through a tiny hole in the door formed by pushing out a knot in the wood. The old woman looked around her, stroked the trunk of the guava tree, then called out to the girl " Tell your mother I am a social worker, and I will come here on this same day next week. " She's coming back" whispered the young girl, her face transformed with joy.

Some time later her mother returned and the young girl related the incident. "She is a great old lady, will she cure me?" she asked her mother in a tearful voice.

"If this girl gets cured, I will be making the liquor, we will have to find her a husband, get her a dowry. Oh no, oh no, none of this curing business" she thought, but aloud she said "she will not come back". But the social worker returned again and again.

"What? you want to get your back straightened? You want to go to a hospital for this? These people are going to teach you an income generating trade?". Each question was accompanied by blows the woman struck on her young daughter's deformed hunched-back. The girl cowered in a corner covering her head with her hands, her forearms bent in front of her face to protect it from the wild hits as she tried to shield her back by pressing herself against the wall. The mother caught her by the arm and threw her on the floor, then picking up a log of firewood, began the beating in earnest. Hearing the cries, the father ran in from the field. His feet and hands were caked with mud, sweat poured down his face and his eyes blazed with fury as they absorbed the scene in the single room of the tiny hut. In one stride he reached his wife and pulled the wood from her hand". "Woman, have you lost your mind? Have you forgotten they are coming to fetch the booze this evening? Have you forgotten the money they will pay? You know she makes the best booze in this *gram sabha,* then why are you trying to bend her back even more than it is already bent? Go girl, get to work. You will wash and rest your back after the booze is in the bottles".

The demand for alcohol increased with the onset of winter and the young girl was busier than ever but one day the mother asked the social worker who was again at their door "what is it that you want?". "I want nothing" replied the old woman "but if you all want something let us discuss the matter". Participatory rural appraisal commenced. The lack of fuel and fodder being uppermost in the woman minds, the discussions inevitably turned to planting and then to the types of fuel and fodder trees the villagers found best suited to their terrain. The discussion on fodder trees became heated and one of the two men who had accompanied the social worker said "Let us play a game" and commenced smoothening an earthen patch simultaneously smoothing ruffled feathers. The game commenced. "Call my cow" said Sumiti Devi the matriarch of the hamlet. "You always ask what we want and what we think, so when you are talking about fodder you should address the cow" she reasoned. The two young men heartily laughed but they agreed, and requested Sumiti Devi to interpret for them. The PRA game, to result in a matrix scoring for fodder species commenced, but the social worker drew aside the young hunch backed girl's mother. By gentle probing she learned, that the girl was the only child, and the mother could have no more children. "Think to the future" she begged. "This child has no means of earning a livelihood! She can never marry! What will be her ultimate fate? I suggest that while she is undergoing therapy let her learn some income generating skill so that at least she has a means of livelihood to support her through life". "How much will she earn per week and what will be the cost of the raw material?" asked the mother flatly. The social worker gasped with astonishment "we have not yet even discussed the skill to be taught, so how can I reply?"

"We'll see, let us think, let me discuss this at home" replied the mother.

"Mother, father," begged the young girl at night after the meagre supper had been consumed, "Please let me go to this hospital to get cured and to learn to earn money". Her father who had imbibed a bottle of the liquor she had made, hit her across the mouth. "Do not use your tongue to talk rubbish or I will cut it out. Go, it is time to go to the hamlet by the spring to deliver two bottles. Don't let him see your deformity. He will run away, you are a young girl he will pay more if you ask him. Carry three bottles in case others come".

The young girl went out in the deepening dusk. She had tucked leaves between the bottles to prevent breakage or clinking, and as she walked slowly along the path she wondered how much more the man would pay if she asked him. The man was already there. He took all three bottles at the usual rate and then on her request he gave her three rupees extra to buy something for herself, but as he walked away he spat on the ground and recited a mantra.

The young girl was overjoyed. She hurried home and gave the entire amount to her father. "Ha!, In future you will also do the selling. Don't be in such a hurry to get rid of your humped back, you will earn more with it than without it."

Meanwhile, in another hamlet of the village occupied by the high caste, all PRA exercises kept coming around to sending the young hunchback for treatment. "It is so sad to see such deformity" said one of the women wiping her eyes and sighing. The social worker agreed and commented that it was doubly sad since the girl had such a beautiful face. "Oh"! The women gasped in horror "she must go for treatment, you must make her mother agree". After the social worker left, the women looked at each other with determination "She goes for training permanently" they unanimously decided. All their husbands drank the alcohol supplied by the girl of the low-caste hamlet and recently they had found their husbands were paying more and more per bottle.

The young hunch-backed girl and the social worker were at the Vocational Training Centre. "Only ten rupees per day?" The young girl queried "Only fifteen rupees a day?" the young girl was remarkably astute when it came to talk about money and so the social worker discussed each course in detail, but the girl found none of them suitable.

"We should tell the old woman what trade the hunchback follows" said one of the upper caste women as she and her friends walked out to cut grass. "No, village talk is village talk we cannot tell her" was the general consensus.

Some weeks passed. Much work had been accomplished in the village the only failure remained the condition of the young girl. Then tragedy struck. There was an outbreak of typhoid and although a doctor and his team managed to control the epidemic, two deaths occurred—the parents of the young girl.

Several days later when the social worker found spare time to think of the young girl's future she hurried to the hut with some fruit and vegetables for she was anxious about the very existence of the child apart from ensuring that she learned a trade, now most urgent.

The social worker found that the hut had already been occupied by the girl's aunt, and was informed that the girl was working in a shack behind the hut. The social worker walked around to the back to meet the young girl.

"My dear child", she whispered as she bent to examine the girl lying unconscious on the floor of the tiny space in which the equipment and storage bin for alcoholic drinks were kept.

A brief examination showed that the girl was drunk. The social worker ran back to the main hut, calling out to the aunt who stepped into the courtyard to meet her. "The child, the child has been drinking herself into a stupor with country liquor! How on earth has this happened?", gasped the social worker.

"Ah!", replied the aunt "the silly girl wanted to learn how to sew in order to earn money, because she wanted to stop making alcohol".

"What? are you telling me that she has been making illicit liquor all this time and no one told me?". "You never asked! Anyway I have solved the problem by making her drink it herself. It has been a waste of money for me, but now I think the girl is addicted so she will never drop this trade. It's a good trade. There's money in it and we give her food and some of the liquor to drink as wages".

"Oh no, you can't do this to her"

"What? a miserable cursed hunchback and you get angry because we feed her? Come everyone listen, listen to this injustice . . ."

The social worker walked sadly back to the roadhead. "If only, if only I had probed deep enough, how different the outcome would have been" she murmured. "All poverty is relative and its alleviation is relative to the prevailing circumstances. Under PRA the women have discussed nothing but money in terms of cash payment for work or in terms of kind, even environmental benefits have been ultimately reckoned in terms of cash benefits, but what did I do about the PRA of ethical values that must form an integral part of development?". Probing would have made me analyse the strange smell that surrounded the child. No wonder the women of the richer hamlet were so anxious to have her taught a trade. They were desperate to stop this drink supply. I should have listened, analysed, reflected, and gently probed, probed . . . Even if I am late, I too have a code of ethics, so today I commence the PRA of ethics, ethics and illicit distilling, ethics and the malformed, ethics and child education, ethics and robbing the environment of its wealth, ethics and a legacy of disaster? . . .

ORGANIZATIONAL CAPACITY BUILDING

13

ORGANIZATIONAL CAPACITY BUILDING FOR PARTICIPATORY RURAL APPRAISAL (PRA)

Some Lessons from the Field

— NEELA MUKHERJEE

It is not enough to change policy paradigm at the policy level for enunciating participatory development as an objective of plans and programmes. It is also equally important to build capacity of development organizations for participatory learning and action. Whereas, the former or the "change in policy paradigm" is a necessary condition, the latter or the "capacity building of development organization" is also another necessary condition for adopting and sustaining participatory approach to development interventions. It is often observed that, despite change in development paradigm at the policy level, participatory approach does not get translated into actual practice in relation to both "inside" and "outside" spheres of development organizations. The inside story of "change" within organization is as much important as "change" in its external sphere of activities. This is because conventional attitude and behaviour of development organizations, internal to them, act as major stumbling blocks for adopting participatory approach to development. The main issue is how organizational change can be brought about so that policy framework on participatory development gets translated into actual practice.

This paper discusses selected issues in capacity building of development organizations for introducing and adapting behavioural change appropriate for practising Participatory Rural Appraisal (PRA). The paper outlines broad phases in participatory learning for assimilation of behavioural change within organizations and looks into ways of sustaining such change. Such broad phases have been identified over time, from observing a few organizations, both governmental and non-governmental, which are trying to adapt to the changing paradigm of development. The phases, observed in general, are described below, although all organizations need not experience all the phases.

The Phases are :

- — Constructing and adopting a framework for participatory learning;
- — Harnessing of organizational support-inside/outside;
- — Organizing participation and sustaining it; and
- — Strengthening interim and post-participation support system for continuity.

Due to many factors such as change in policy or leadership an organization may not experience all the phases over time and a phase once started can also end abruptly due to unforeseen changes. Such phases can occur as a sequence in an organization or selected phases, especially the last two, can occur simultaneously in an organization. It has also been observed that the phases can be widely different in different divisions/units of the same organization which decide to change. The time duration of each phase would differ across organizations, behavioural change, any way, is a time-consuming process. Similarly the quality of behavioural change would also tend to differ across organizations.

I. Constructing and Adopting a Framework

Constructing an organizational framework appropriate to the changing paradigm of development sets the pace for organizing a frame of reference for undertaking changes in philosophy and approach to development through objectives, methodologies and strategies. Such framework can be either handed down from "above" through policy guidelines of the State or given by a donor/head organization or alternatively evolved at the organizational level. Some of the relevant issues for constructing an organizational framework for pursuing participatory development are as follows.

- — Why should an organization change its existing approach towards participatory learning and action?

— What would be the dimensions of that change framework which an organization would be required to adapt?
— How is it different from the existing system?
— What are the new principles to follow and what objectives to attain?
— How does an organization inculcate participation-friendly attitude and behaviour?

One core issue, in this context is that of creating a suitable framework for adopting PRA. Such a framework can be drawn from the emerging paradigm of "constructivist realism", borrowed from other institutions or adapted from institutional experience in field-level development. The principles, objectives, methodology, process and evaluation of PRA-type activities are all parts of that framework. The principles are based on right attitude and behaviour in organizing participation. The foremost principles are that of listening and learning from the people and not lecturing, offsetting spatial, temporal and people's biases by approaching remote areas in difficult seasons, and interacting with deprived, weak and marginalised groups. In all respects, it is seeking diversity of people, process, methods and time and thereby reinforcing participatory learning experience.

Here the problem arises with "our" organizational attitude and behaviour which are influenced by the system in which developmental activities ,take place. The philosophy of the system is a major determinant of attitude and behaviour for those involved in planning and executing developmental projects. In the conventional system based on 'development from above', one underlying assumption is that people from "below" or at the local level, are ignorant, not concerned and not capable of taking decisions concerning their well-being. The other assumption is that "ourselves" from "above" have the required skills and knowledge concerning local development and have ready-made solutions to local problems, irrespective of local factors.

Attitude and behaviour of "ourselves", influenced by such assumptions of the system tend towards those of "givers from above", where the people are "takers from below". By virtue of "our" decision-making position and control over resources, "we" tend to dominate the scene of development, being aware of "our" superior position in the system and "our" power to "give" while maintaining that the people are in an inferior position for it is they who "receive". In the presence of conventional attitude and behaviour a development organization is handicapped to learn about the following,

— about client/stakeholders' reality for professional's worldview is limited;
— about how to get better response from grassroot;
— about ways for better understanding and management of projects;
— about ways for sustainability of interventions through community involvement; and
— about methods for deriving professional satisfaction for organizational performance.

It is important that a process of change is initiated in the conventional attitude and behaviour of development organizations by means of a framework for participatory development. The objective of PRA is people's empowerment for greater and better involvement of local communities for development activities, by seeking their view, knowledge, perceptions, experience, contributions and active involvement as stakeholders in the process of development. The spirit of sharing is an integral part of that framework. The change envisaged is the change in attitude and behaviour of development workers in understanding and appreciating people's reality. The principles, objectives, methods, process and evaluation — all reflect creation and sustenance of participation and reinforce each other to have a synergistic impact on participatory development.

II. Harnessing Organizational Support

The organizations in a changing trajectory, need to clarify their objectives and roles. It is an evolutionary process in which an organization can learn from its own experience or from other organizations and share such experience within and amongst themselves. Ultimately, for strengthening organizational support, the organizations need to restructure themselves towards pursuing participatory learning and action in their agenda for development. The changing role of organizations from "administrators", "implementors to "facilitators" is a crucial step towards sustaining capacity building in participatory development.

With the framework for participatory development, as given above, it is an advantage if there emerge some "leaders" in introducing the changed framework of development into actual practice following which others can emulate. Organizational support from headquarters is most often required by field/branch offices for translating ideas into action.

Some "lead" institutions which are able to influence their organizational attitude and behaviour can show way to others. Not all institutions have the same flexibility for acting as agents of change. Some would lead while others would follow. Those of which are dynamic, flexible and willing to accept new ideas and innovations can be leaders in the field to bring about changes in attitude and behaviour as envisaged.

III. Organizing and Sustaining Participation

To begin with, the new objectives of people's empowerment and changed role of organizations as "facilitators" of development would help to create a transparent process in organizing participatory learning. This phase can actually evolve depending on learning at each stage. Changes in attitude and behaviour can be initiated through training- workshops. Undoubtedly, training is a powerful way of influencing human behaviour, however, there are other ways as well and organizations can remain flexible enough to innovate and adopt different ways for influencing human behaviour.

Some ways to influence human behaviour are,

— training,
— building teams of motivated individuals,
— encouraging peer-group/mixed group interactions,
— forming informal learning groups,
— holding workshops with extended groups like communities/ other institutions,
— arranging periodic participatory 'clinics',
— mentoring by seniors,
— competing by small groups,
— imitating role models,
— inculcating self-learning from field, and
— providing incentives and rewards from within and outside.

To start with, quality-oriented training in PRA-type activities can initiate a process of change in attitude and behaviour of an organization, which the organization can attempt to sustain through proper motivation of its staff to improve upon individual and group performance. Such motivation can be provided at different levels and in different ways for all levels of organizational staff. Brain-storming by staff on field-level realities of that organization would help it to evolve suitable strategy/ strategies for translating participatory philosophy into action in field situations.

At the beginning, training-workshops accompanied by field-visits can provide opportunities for influencing attitude and behaviour of an organization. However, there can arise the need for having more than one round of PRA training- workshop since PRA-type activities often require reinforcement of learning from time to time. It is not difficult to discover different categories of trainees with differential training needs and it is important to recognise such diverse categories of needs, Quality-oriented training in PRA-type activities can initiate changes in attitudes and behaviour, which, however, can be sustained, amongst others, through proper motivation to improve upon individual/ group performance. Such motivating forces to an individual member of an organization can be provided by seniors, peer groups and juniors, other groups, field-level realities, and through one's own self. Self-propelled learning from the field is a powerful way of inculcating the desired attitudes and behaviour in PRA-type activities. With change in individual member's approach the attitude and behaviour of that organization also get influenced. In this context, some of the do's for individuals as members of organization are listed below.

Doables in Individual's Attitude and Behaviour

— Listen and learn;
— Respect others, also be worthy of their respect;
— Learn about own strength and weaknesses;
— Build on diversity of experience;
— Build networks and effective channels of communication with partner and other agencies;
— Have reinforcement of training from time to time;
— Be pro-active;
— Take initiative;
— Meet people informally;
— Start small, others can join later;
— Have confidence; and
— Remember it is essentially learning-by-doing.

Organizations can build teams of motivated individuals with different sets of strength in planning and execution of developmental projects. Peer-groups can meet often for informal interactions and sharing of views. Informal learning groups, small in size, cutting across different layers of an organization can highlight issues from different perspectives and discuss them. Learning groups can cut across similar other organizations and local communities. PRA 'clinics' can bring to fore many issues from time to time and discuss ways of resolving them. Such 'clinics' play a useful role in conflict-resolution and in strengthening the process of learning.

In mentoring, a close relationship with a senior staff of proven behaviour and skill is likely to keep a young staff open and yearning for growth. Institutions can nurture such relationship by assigning mentors to junior staff members. The mentor needs to create effective channels of communication, inspire and instil values in the junior, encourage positive attitudes, and discourage cynicism and negative attitudes in the junior. This would increase the confidence of junior staff who is being mentored, open channels of communication and influence way of thinking of that staff and thereby create opportunities for attitudinal change.

Some people would change their attitudes and behaviour after observing others in actual practice. Teams of junior and senior staff in field work can also help to influence attitudes and behaviour in case such teams operate on the basis of democratic values. Long field work and travel help in forging personal relationship and lead to better understanding and team work. Sometimes incentives and rewards also create supportive environment for appropriate attitude and behaviour.

In any case, organizational heads/leaders play an important role for facilitating the impetus for change. Some of the do's for organizational heads/leaders are listed below.

Some Do's for Organizational Heads/Leaders

— Be interested in developing human resources of your organization; organize training-workshops for staff from time to time.

— Gather diverse experience and attend training-workshops from time to time.

— Be open for innovations and experiments in participation and create conditions for change.

— Give incentives to those field workers who make genuine efforts.

— Learn to embrace errors.

— Try to instil democratic values by practising them, listen to staff.

— Discourage those who obstruct free flow of ideas.

— Try to arrive at a vision with your staff and inspire them.
— Find ways to make rules and procedures flexible so that they do not block decision-making.
— Form small teams of dedicated staff and match persons with jobs.
— Match assignments with proportionate responsibility and accountability.
— Monitor programme samples and share results in a positive manner.
— Visit local communities from the field and learn from them.
— Encourage workshops with local communities and other organizations.
— Try to network with other parallel organizations and have joint sessions for brain-storming on common issues
— Decentralise decision-making amongst your staff and make arrangements for attending to mundane requirements of field workers.

IV. Interim and Post-Participation Support System

During the process of participatory learning, there can arise different issues at different stages which may require internal and/or external support. The process of participatory learning has its own momentum, in terms of time and progress and would differ across organizations depending on their adaptability, determination and perceived needs. At each stage, diverse ways of strengthening such learning becomes important. New and uncommon issues can arise which require immediate attention for amicable resolution through mutual discussion and brain-storming. The issues can be focussed upon through training-workshops, seminars, joint sessions for discussion and consultation with stakeholders, peer group meetings and others.

It is important for any organization, embarking on the path of PRA-type activities, to either build a support system in its own way or to have access to it as and when required. This is all the more important because PRA-type activity is essentially learning-by-doing and there are many unknown factors, concepts issues and situations which cannot be comprehended from the beginning. The support system can be referred to for looking at problematic issues, for identifying concealed factors and, if possible, suggesting ways to overcome them. Such a system can consist of groups of experienced individuals drawn from different organizations including local level organizations and community institutions and neutral observers, who are willing to lend a helping hand and/or have some stakes/interest in the concerned organizations's path of participatory development.

The four broad phases described above for influencing organizational behaviour are also subject to external environment within which such development organizations operate. Factors like policy-environment, donor's agenda, time horizon, availability of resources, commitment of leadership, autonomy and scope for flexible operations etc. are important determinants which can pose limits to participatory learning and action of organizations.

In an era of "development from below", the conventional attitudes and behaviour pose as stumbling blocks for adapting to changing realities and new ways of thinking about developmental issues. It is being increasingly realised that the earlier capacities built for bringing changes through "development from above" are no longer relevant in the current development scenario. The paradigmatic shift in developmental thinking from absolute assertions to the realities of community participation and empowerment warrant appropriate capacity building of those organizations entrusted with the task of organizing and facilitating developmental activities. It is in this context, that PRA-type activities imply organizational change in conventional attitude and behaviour as a pre-requisite for participatory learning and action. And, it is here that developmental organizations need to identify appropriate strategies for bringing about organizational change without which participatory learning and action cannot be translated into reality.

INDEX